# Quartet of Poems

**Modern Women Writers**

Series editor: Maura Healy

*The Albatross and Other Stories* Susan Hill
*Bitter Medicine* Sara Paretsky
*City of Illusions* Ursula Le Guin
*Cover Her Face* P D James
*Edith Jackson* Rosa Guy
*Fiela's Child* Dalene Matthee
*Fire the Sun* an anthology of poems
*Heartstones* Ruth Rendell
*Heat and Dust* Ruth Prawer Jhabvala
*Hotel du Lac* Anita Brookner
*My Brilliant Career* Miles Franklin
*Not Not Not Not Not Enough Oxygen and Other Plays* Caryl Churchill
*Quartet of Stories* Maya Angelou, Lorna Goodison, Olive Senior, Alice Walker
*Quartet of Poems* Maya Angelou, Lorna Goodison, Grace Nichols, Alice Walker
*The Storyteller* a collection of short stories by Maeve Binchy
*Tales for the Telling* a collection of short stories

# Quartet of Poems

*edited by*

**Maura Healy**

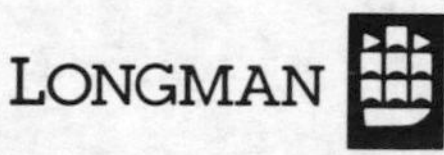

Longman Group UK Limited,
*Longman House, Burnt Mill, Harlow,*
*Essex CM20 2JE, England*
*and Associated Companies throughout the world.*



First published 1993

*Set in 10/12 point Baskerville, Linotron 202*
*Produced by Longman Singapore Publishers (Pte) Ltd*
*Printed in Singapore*

*ISBN 0 582 08299 4*

**To my mother, Mary. 'May I inherit half her strength.'**

# Contents

*How this book is arranged* viii

*Introduction* ix
The poets ix
The poets' backgrounds x
The poems xii

*A Quartet of Poems* 1
**Maya Angelou** 3
Phenomenal Woman 4
Still I Rise 6
The Memory 8
When I Think About Myself 9
Coleridge Jackson 10
Why Are They Happy People? 13
Equality 14
Remembrance 16
Now Long Ago 17
**Alice Walker** 19
Remember? 20
Well 22
Early Losses: a Requiem 26
Johann 33
Did This Happen to Your Mother? Did Your Sister Throw Up a Lot? 36
Gift 38
At First 39
Mississippi Winter IV 40
In These Dissenting Times 40
Women 41
Poem at Thirty-Nine 42
For My Sister Molly Who in the Fifties 44
I Said to Poetry 48

**Grace Nichols** 51
From dih pout 52
Taint 53
One Continent / To Another 54
We the Women 57
Ala 58
Sugar Cane 60
Love Act 64
Skin-Teeth 66
I Coming Back 67
In My Name 68
Epilogue 70
Holding My Beads 70
Between Women 71
Of course when they ask for poems about the 'Realities' of black women 72
Dust 75
The Body Reclining 76
Because She Has Come 78
On Stars 79
Tapestry 79
Beauty 80
Afterword 81
Praise Song for My Mother 82
**Lorna Goodison** 83
My Last Poem 84
Songs For My Son 87
Mulatta Song – II 90
The Mulatta as Penelope 91
We Are the Women 92
I Am Becoming My Mother 94
For My Mother (May I Inherit Half Her Strength) 95
For Rosa Parks 99
Bedspread 100
Some of My Worst Wounds 102
O Love You So Fear the Dark 103

Farewell Wild Woman (I) 104
Farewell Wild Woman (II) 105
Always Homing Now Soul Towards Light 106

*Notes to help your reading* 108

*Now you have read the poems* 114
Keeping a reading log 114
Building up your own poetry anthology 114

*Coursework assignments* 115
Oral assignments 115
Assignments on each group of poems 118
Assignments on the whole anthology 146

*Wider reading* 151
Assignments based on wider reading 152

# How this book is arranged

The most important section of this book contains the pages of poetry, but the material which surrounds the poems is designed to help you get the most out of them.

The Introduction gives you an insight into the poets and their concerns. The section called 'Notes to help your reading' on page 108 explains words, phrases and ideas which may be new to you. The 'Coursework assignments' which follow on page 115 will help you to consider each poet separately and then to think about them together. This material has been carefully planned to support your work towards GCSE. It is written in such a way that you can work through it by yourself, with a friend or in a small group in your class, or with your teacher.

# Introduction

## *The poets*

Two of these poets are very well known. You may have heard of or read Alice Walker's novel *The Colour Purple* and Maya Angelou's series of autobiographical novels which starts with *I Know Why The Caged Bird Sings*. Grace Nichols and Lorna Goodison may not be such familiar names, but a glance at their powerful poetry will explain why they are here.

The four poets have some things in common. All are women, all are black and their poems blend like the different voices in a choir as they celebrate their roots. Each has a distinctive voice and a distinctive experience. They won't allow you to fit them into a stereotype as Grace Nichols says in her poem 'Of course when they ask for poems about the "Realities" of black women':

still there ain't no
easy belly category

for a black woman
or a white woman
or a green woman

and there are black women
strong and eloquent
and focussed

and there are black women
who somehow always manage to end up
frail victim

and there are black women
considered so dangerous
in South Africa
they prison them away

maybe this poem is to say

that I like to see
we black women
full-of-we-selves walking
(pages 73–4)

These poets are defiant, aggressive, tender and humorous as they reflect on their lives, their culture and their relationships. We see into their world and in doing so enrich our understanding of our own world.

## *The poets' backgrounds*

### Maya Angelou

She was born in St Louis, Missouri in 1928. Her novels trace her own story. After the break up of her parents' marriage, she went to live with her grandmother. At the age of eight she was raped by her mother's boyfriend and as a result became mute – she did not speak again for five years. When she was sixteen she had a baby, her son Guy.

Maya Angelou is a woman of many talents; as well as being a prolific writer she has been a waitress, singer, dancer, actress – earning what she could, how she could, to support herself and her child. She has also been very active in black politics. Her autobiography consists of five volumes: *I Know Why The Caged Bird Sings, Gather Together In My Name, Singin' and Swingin'* and *Getting Merry Like Christmas, The Heart of a Woman* and *All God's Children Need Travelling Shoes*. She has published a number of volumes of poetry from which the poems in this anthology have been chosen. Her collections are: *And Still I Rise, Just Give Me a Cool Drink of Water 'Fore I Die* and *I Shall Not Be Moved.* All her novels and poetry are published by Virago.

Maya Angelou is now Reynolds Professor of American Studies at Wake Forest University in North Carolina, USA.

## Alice Walker

She was born in Eatonton, Georgia. Her novels include *The Colour Purple* which won the Pulitzer Prize for literature, *The Temple Of My Familiar, Meridan* and *The Third Life of Grange Copeland*. She has published two volumes of short stories, *In Love and Trouble* and *You Can't Keep a Good Woman Down* and four volumes of poetry from which the poems in this anthology are selected: *Horses Make a Landscape, Look More Beautiful, Once, Revolutionary Returnias* and *Good Night Willie Lee, I'll See You In The Morning*. She has also published a prose collection *In Search of Our Mothers' Gardens*. All these are published by The Women's Press.

Alice Walker is consulting editor to the feminist monthly journal *Ms* and to *Freedom Ways*, a black political magazine.

## Grace Nichols

She was born in 1950 in Georgetown, Guyana, where she grew up and worked as a journalist. She came to live in Britain in 1977. Grace Nichols has written a number of children's books including a volume of poetry, *Come On In To My Tropical Garden*, and a collection of stories *Trust You Wriggly*, both published by Hodder and Stoughton. She has also written *Baby Fish and Other Stories*, folk tales illustrated by her ten-year-old daughter, which she published herself. Her novel for adults, *Whole of a Morning*, is published by Virago.

Her poetry includes *i is a long memoried woman*. This collection won the Commonwealth Poetry Prize and is published by Karnac House which specialises in Caribbean writing. Virago publishes two other volumes: *The Fat Black Woman's Poems* and *Lazy Thoughts of a Lazy Woman*. Her poems appear in a number of other anthologies, including *A Dangerous Knowing*, a collection of poetry from four black writers published by Sheba.

### Lorna Goodison

She was born in Kingston, Jamaica and still lives there with her son Miles. She has published an anthology of stories in Longman's Caribbean Series, *Baby Mother and the King of Swords*. Her poetry collections include: *Tamarind Season* (Institute of Jamaica Publishers) and *I Am Becoming My Mother* and *Heartease* both published by New Beacon Press.

Goodison is a painter as well as a poet. Of her writing she said in an interview with *The Guardian* in 1985: 'I am a poet, but I didn't choose poetry – it chose me . . . it's a dominating, intrusive tyrant. It's something I have to do – a wicked force.' Her poems are so beautiful that we must be grateful that poetry chose her.

## *The poems*

### They emerge 'so fine'

Poetry is different from prose. Here is how Lorna Goodison describes the job of the poet in this extract from 'My Last Poem'.

I once wrote poems
that emerged so fine
with a rough edge for honing
a soft cloth for polishing
and a houseproud eye
I'd pride myself in making them shine.

(page 84)

She sees herself almost like a sculptor, making a rough outline and then shaping and refining the piece until it shines.

Much of the pleasure we get from reading poems comes from our delight in the care, the skill, the instinct of the poet in choosing this word not that, grouping the words, balancing them so that they are polished and perfect, so that they communicate to us. Of course, we have to listen carefully if we are to hear what the poet has to say and to enjoy how she says it. We may need to hear or read a poem more than once if we are to appreciate it fully. Poems are not to be eaten in one gulp but to be savoured!

## They make us see things differently

We can be surprised and delighted by some of the unusual connections poets make when they link different ideas. The imagery Grace Nichols uses in this short poem is a good example of a delightful link.

*On Stars*

Stars are the nipples
of angels
pressed against the face
of heaven.

(page 79)

## They are best read aloud

A good example of this is Maya Angelou's poetry which is at its best when it is presented as a performance – read out loud to stress its rhythms. She reads with the confidence of an actress and a great sense of delight in her words. Imagine her on stage reading this:

*Phenomenal Woman*

Pretty women wonder where my secret lies.
I'm not cute or built to suit a fashion model's size
But when I start to tell them,

They think I'm telling lies.
I say,
It's in the reach of my arms,
The span of my hips,
The stride of my step,
The curl of my lips.
I'm a woman
Phenomenally.
Phenomenal woman,
That's me.

(page 4)

All the poems in this collection should be read aloud to be fully enjoyed. Let the shape of the line and the verse guide the rhythm of your reading. If you find a poem difficult, then reading it aloud will help 'unlock' it, because it has been written to be spoken and heard. Try reading Alice Walker's poem 'Remember?' (page 20) to enjoy the way it works when spoken out loud.

## They record moments of insight or emotion

We hurtle on through busy lives and it's often hard to stop and really look or really feel. Poems stop us in our tracks. Writing poetry makes us delve into our minds and hearts and find the words to talk about important feelings, ideas or experiences. Alice Walker's poem 'I Said to Poetry' (page 48) is an imaginary argument with Poetry. She is trying to resist the impulse to write.

I said to Poetry: 'I'm finished
with you.'
Having to almost die
before some weird light
comes creeping through
is no fun . . .

but Poetry woke her up at five in the morning with the germ of an idea for a poem. She wants to go back to sleep but Poetry argues with her:

Poetry said: 'But think about the time
you saw the moon
over the small canyon
that you liked much better
than the grand one – and how surprised you were
that the moonlight was green
and you still had
one good eye
to see it with...

Walker tries to think of excuses not to write. She has no paper, she doesn't like her pen:

'Bullshit,' said Poetry.
'Bullshit,' said I.

In an amusing way the poem raises the problem that poetry is often disturbing, that in writing and reading it we 'plug in' to deep emotions.

## They have three common themes

These poems:

- trace the roots of black people;
- are defiant and celebratory;
- value women.

### *Tracing roots*

Nichols' poem 'Epilogue' explores this theme. In a few words she records how people were taken across the ocean to be sold as slaves and how they were robbed of their roots as well as their freedom. From this pain and loss a new sense of identity and culture has emerged.

I have crossed an ocean
I have lost my tongue
From the root of the old
one
a new one has sprung
(page 70)

*Defiant and celebratory*

All four poets speak with a new tongue. Instead of seeing themselves and their forebears as victims, they celebrate their survival and their ability to withstand and even triumph over repression. Here's how Nichols describes this process:

*Skin-Teeth*

Not every skin-teeth
is a smile 'Massa'
if you see me smiling
when you pass

if you see me bending
when you ask

Know that I smile
know that I bend
only the better
to rise and strike
again
(page 66)

*Valuing women*

The poets featured in this collection write from their own experience. They speak of finding strength and vision in themselves and of gaining strength from other women. They celebrate women's achievements in the public world, and the private world of the family. They recognise the strength of their sisters and friends and mothers and give thanks, like Goodison in:

*For My Mother (May I Inherit Half Her Strength)*

For her hands grown coarse with raising nine children
for her body for twenty years permanently fat
for the time she pawned her machine for my sister's
Senior Cambridge fees
and for the pain she bore with the eyes of a queen...

(page 98)

These poems speak of extraordinary women like Rosa Parks whose refusal to give up a seat on a bus to a white person started the American Civil Rights Movement. They speak also of ordinary women and this is what makes them so fresh and so exciting. We recognise these people as being like us and our family and friends and we learn there is poetry in us all.

# Quartet of Poems

# Maya Angelou

## *Phenomenal Woman*

Pretty women wonder where my secret lies.
I'm not cute or built to suit a fashion model's size
But when I start to tell them,
They think I'm telling lies.
I say,
It's in the reach of my arms,
The span of my hips,
The stride of my step,
The curl of my lips.
I'm a woman
Phenomenally.
Phenomenal woman,
That's me.

I walk into a room
Just as cool as you please,
And to a man,
The fellows stand or
Fall down on their knees.
Then they swarm around me,
A hive of honey bees.
I say,
It's the fire in my eyes,
And the flash of my teeth,
The swing in my waist,
And the joy in my feet.
I'm a woman
Phenomenally.
Phenomenal woman,
That's me.

Men themselves have wondered
What they see in me.
They try so much
But they can't touch
My inner mystery.
When I try to show them
They say they still can't see.
I say,
It's in the arch of my back,
The sun of my smile,
The ride of my breasts,
The grace of my style.
I'm a woman
Phenomenally.
Phenomenal woman,
That's me.

Now you understand
Just why my head's not bowed.
I don't shout or jump about
Or have to talk real loud.
When you see me passing
It ought to make you proud.
I say,
It's in the click of my heels,
The bend of my hair,
the palm of my hand,
The need for my care.
'Cause I'm a woman
Phenomenally.
Phenomenal woman,
That's me.

## *Still I Rise*

You may write me down in history
With your bitter, twisted lies,
You may trod me in the very dirt
But still, like dust, I'll rise.

Does my sassiness upset you?
Why are you beset with gloom?
'Cause I walk like I've got oil wells
Pumping in my living room.

Just like moons and like suns,
With the certainty of tides,
Just like hopes springing high,
Still I'll rise.

Did you want to see me broken?
Bowed head and lowered eyes?
Shoulders falling down like teardrops,
Weakened by my soulful cries.

Does my haughtiness offend you?
Don't you take it awful hard
'Cause I laugh like I've got gold mines
Diggin' in my own back yard.

You may shoot me with your words,
You may cut me with your eyes,
You may kill me with your hatefulness,
But still, like air, I'll rise.

Does my sexiness upset you?
Does it come as a surprise
That I dance like I've got diamonds
At the meeting of my thighs?

Out of the huts of history's shame
I rise
Up from a past that's rooted in pain
I rise
I'm a black ocean, leaping and wide,
Welling and swelling I bear in the tide.

Leaving behind nights of terror and fear
I rise
Into a daybreak that's wondrously clear
I rise
Bringing the gifts that my ancestors gave,
I am the dream and the hope of the slave.
I rise
I rise
I rise.

## *The Memory*

Cotton rows crisscross the world
And dead-tired nights of yearning
Thunderbolts on leather strops
And all my body burning

Sugar cane reach up to God
And every baby crying
Shame the blanket of my night
And all my days are dying

## *When I Think About Myself*

When I think about myself,
I almost laugh myself to death,
My life has been one great big joke,
A dance that's walked
A song that's spoke,
I laugh so hard I almost choke
When I think about myself.

Sixty years in these folks' world
The child I works for calls me girl
I say 'Yes ma'am' for working's sake.
Too proud to bend
Too poor to break,
I laugh until my stomach ache,
When I think about myself.

My folks can make me split my side,
I laughed so hard I nearly died,
The tales they tell, sound just like lying,
They grow the fruit,
But eat the rind,
I laugh until I start to crying,
When I think about my folks.

## *Coleridge Jackson*

Coleridge Jackson had nothing
to fear. He weighed sixty pounds
more than his sons and one
hundred pounds more than his wife.

His neighbors knew he wouldn't
take tea for the fever.
The gents at the poolroom
walked gently in his presence.

So everyone used
to wonder why,
when his puny boss, a little
white bag of bones and
squinty eyes, when he frowned
at Coleridge, sneered at
the way Coleridge shifted
a ton of canned goods from
the east wall of the warehouse
all the way to the west,
when that skimpy piece of
man-meat called Coleridge
a sorry nigger,
Coleridge kept his lips closed,
sealed, jammed tight.
Wouldn't raise his eyes,
held his head at a slant,
looking way off somewhere
else.

Everybody in the neighborhood wondered
why Coleridge would come home,
pull off his jacket, take off
his shoes, and beat the
water and the will out of his puny
little family.

Everybody, even Coleridge, wondered
(the next day, or even later that
same night).
Everybody. But the weasly little
sack-of-bones boss with his
envious little eyes,
he knew. He always
knew. And
when people told him about
Coleridge's family, about the
black eyes and the bruised
faces, the broken bones,
Lord, how that scrawny man
grinned.

And the next
day, for a few hours, he treated
Coleridge nice. Like Coleridge
had just done him the biggest
old favor. Then, right
after lunch, he'd start on
Coleridge again.

'Here, Sambo, come here.
Can't you move any faster
than that? Who on earth
needs a lazy nigger?'
And Coleridge would just
stand there. His eyes sliding
away, lurking at something else.

## *Why Are They Happy People?*

Skin back your teeth, damn you,
wiggle your ears,
laugh while the years
race
down your face.

Pull up your cheeks, black boy,
wrinkle your nose,
grin as your toes
spade
up your grave.

Roll those big eyes, black gal,
rubber your knees,
smile when the trees
bend
with your kin.

## *Equality*

You declare you see me dimly
through a glass which will not shine,
though I stand before you boldly,
trim in rank and marking time.

You do own to hear me faintly
as a whisper out of range,
while my drums beat out the message
and the rhythms never change.

Equality, and I will be free.
Equality, and I will be free.

You announce my ways are wanton,
that I fly from man to man,
but if I'm just a shadow to you,
could you ever understand?

We have lived a painful history,
we know the shameful past,
but I keep on marching forward,
and you keep on coming last.

Equality, and I will be free.
Equality, and I will be free.

Take the blinders from your vision,
take the padding from your ears,
and confess you've heard me crying,
and admit you've seen my tears.

Hear the tempo so compelling,
hear the blood throb in my veins.
Yes, my drums are beating nightly,
and the rhythms never change.

Equality, and I will be free.
Equality, and I will be free.

## *Remembrance*

*for Paul*

Your hands easy
weight, teasing the bees
hived in my hair, your smile at the
slope of my cheek. On the
occasion, you press
above me, glowing, spouting
readiness, mystery rapes
my reason.

When you have withdrawn
your self and the magic, when
only the smell of your
love lingers between
my breasts, then, only
then, can I greedily consume
your presence.

## *Now Long Ago*

One innocent spring
your voice meant to me
less than tires turning
on a distant street.

Your name, perhaps spoken,
led no chorus of
batons
unrehearsed
to crush against my
empty chest.

That cool spring
was shortened by
your summer, bold impatient
and all forgotten
except when silence
turns the key
into my midnight bedroom
and comes to sleep upon your
pillow.

# Alice Walker

## *Remember?*

Remember me?
I am the girl
with the dark skin
whose shoes are thin
I am the girl
with rotted teeth
I am the dark
rotten-toothed girl
with the wounded eye
and the melted ear.

I am the girl
holding their babies
cooking their meals
sweeping their yards
washing their clothes
Dark and rotting
and wounded, wounded.

I would give
to the human race
only hope.

I am the woman
with the blessed
dark skin
I am the woman
with teeth repaired
I am the woman
with the healing eye
the ear that hears.

I am the woman: Dark,
repaired, healed
Listening to you.

I would give
to the human race
only hope.

I am the woman
offering two flowers
whose roots
are twin

Justice and Hope

Let us begin.

## *Well*

Well.

He was a poet
a priest
a revolutionary
compañero
and we were right
to be seduced.

He brought us greetings
from his countrypeople
and informed us
with lifted
fist
that they would not
be moved.

All his poems
were eloquent.

I liked
especially
the one
that said
the revolution
must
liberate
the cougars, the trees,
and the lakes;

when he read it
everyone
breathed
relief;
ecology
lives
of all places
in Central
America!
we thought.

And then he read
a poem
about Grenada
and we
smiled
until he began
to describe
the women:

Well. One woman
when she smiled
had shiny black
lips
which reminded him
of black legs
(vaselined, no doubt),
her whole mouth
to the poet
revolutionary
suddenly
a leg

(and one said
What?)

Another one,
duly noted by
the priest,
apparently
barely attentive
at a political
rally
eating
a mango

Another wears
a red dress,
her breasts
(no kidding!)
like coconuts . . .

Well. Nobody ever said
supporting other people's revolutions
wouldn't make us
ill:

But what a pity
that
the poet
the priest
and the revolution
never seem
to arrive
for the black woman,
herself.

Only for her black lips
or her black leg
does one or the other
arrive;
only for her
devouring mouth
always depicted
in the act
of eating
something colorful

only for her breasts
like coconuts
and her red dress.

## *Early Losses: a Requiem*

### PART I

Nyanu was appointed
as my Lord. The husband chosen
by the elders
before my birth.
He sipped wine with
my father
and when I was born
brought a parrot as
his gift
to play with me.
Paid baskets of grain
and sweet berries
to make me fat
for his pleasure.

Omunu was my playmate
who helped consume
Nyanu's gifts.
Our fat selves grew
together
knee and knee.
It was Omunu I wished
to share my tiny
playing house.

Him I loved as the sun
must seek and chase

its own reflection
across the sky.
My brothers, before you
turn away —

The day the savages came
to ambush our village
it was Nyanu who struggled
bravely
Omunu ran and hid
behind his parents' house.
He was a coward but
only nine
as was I; who trembled
beside him as we two
were stolen away
Nyanu's dead body
begging remembrance
of his tiny morsel
taken from his mouth.
Nor was I joyful that he was dead
only glad that now I would not have
to marry him.

Omunu clasped my hands
within the barkcloth pouch
and I his head
a battered flower
bent low
upon its stalk
Our cries pounded back
into our throats

by thudding blows
we could not see
our mothers' cries
at such a distance
we could not hear
and over the miles
we feasted on homesickness
our mothers' tears and
the dew
all we consumed of homeland
before we left.

At the great water Omunu fought
to stay with me
at such a tender age
our hearts we set
upon each other
as the retreating wave
brings its closest friend
upon its back.
We cried out in words
that met an echo
and Omunu vanished
down a hole that
smelled of blood and
excrement and death
and I was 'saved'
for sport among
the sailors of the crew.
Only nine, upon a ship. My mouth
my body a mystery
that opened with each tearing

lunge. Crying for Omunu
who was not seen
again
by these eyes.

Listen to your sister, singing
in the field.
My body forced to receive
grain and wild berries
and milk so I could seem
a likely wench
— my mother's child
sold for a price. My father's
child again for sale.
I prayed to all our Gods
'Come down to me'
Hoist the burden no child
was meant to bear
and decipher the prayer
from within each song
— the song despised —
my belly become a stronghold
for a stranger
who will not recall
when he is two
the contours of
his mother's face.
See the savages turn back
my lips
and with hot irons
brand me neck and thigh.

I could not see the horizon
for the sky
a burning eye
the sun, beloved in the shade,
became an enemy
a pestle pounding long
upon my head.
You walked with me.
And when day sagged into night
some one of you of my own
choice
shared my rest. Omunu
risen from the ocean
out of the stomachs of whales
the teeth of sharks
lying beside me sleeping
knee and knee.
We could not speak always
of hearts
for in the morning if they
sold you
how could I flatten
a wrinkled face?
The stupor of dread
made smooth the look
that to my tormentors
was born erased.
I mourned for you. And if you died
took out my heart upon my lap
and rested it.

See me old at thirty
my sack of cotton weighted
to the ground. My hair
enough to cover a marble
my teeth like rattles
made of chalk
my breath a whisper
of decay.
The slack of my belly
falling to my knees.
I shrink to become a tiny size
a delicate morsel
upon my mother's knee
prepared like bread. The shimmering
of the sun a noise
upon my head.

To the child that's left
I offer a sound
without a promise
a clue
of what it means.

The sound itself is all.

PART II

## The Child

A sound like a small wind
finding the door of a
hollow reed
my mother's farewell
glocked up from the back
of her throat

*the sound itself is all*

all I have
to remember a mother
I scarcely knew.

'Omunu' to me; who never knew
what 'Omunu' meant. Whether home
or man or trusted God. 'Omunu'.
Her only treasure,
and never spent.

## *Johann*

You look at me with children
In your eyes,
  Blond, blue-eyed
Teutons
Charmingly veiled
In bronze
  Got from me.

What would Hitler say?

I am brown-er
Than a jew
Being one step
Beyond that Colored scene.
You are the Golden Boy,
Shiny but bloody
And with that ancient martial tune
Only your heart is out of step —
You love.

But even knowing love
I shrink from you. Blond
And Black; it is too charged a combination.
Charged with past and present wars,
Charged with frenzy
and with blood
Dare I kiss your German mouth?
Touch the perfect muscles
Underneath the yellow shirt

Blending coolly
With your yellow
Hair?

I shudder at the whiteness
Of your hands.

Blue is too cold a color
For eyes.

But white, I think, is the color
Of honest flowers,

And blue is the color
Of the sky.

Come closer then and hold out to me
Your white and faintly bloodied hands.
I will kiss your German mouth
And will touch the helpless
White skin, gone red,
Beneath the yellow shirt.
I will rock the yellow head against
My breast, brown and yielding.

But I tell you, love,
There is still much to fear.
We have only seen the
First of wars,
First of frenzies
First of blood.

Someday, perhaps, we will be
Made to learn
That blond and black
Cannot love.

But until that rushing day
I will not reject you.
I will kiss your fearful
German mouth.
And you —
Look at me boldly
With surging, brown-blond teutons
In your eyes.

## *Did This Happen to Your Mother? Did Your Sister Throw Up a Lot?*

I love a man who is not worth
my love.
Did this happen to your mother?
Did your grandmother wake up
for no good reason
in the middle of the night?

I thought love could be controlled.
It cannot.
Only behaviour can be controlled.
By biting your tongue purple
rather than speak.
Mauling your lips.
Obliterating his number
too thoroughly
to be able to phone.

Love has made me sick.

Did your sister throw up a lot?
Did your cousin complain
of a painful knot
in her back?
Did your aunt always
seem to have something else
troubling her mind?

I thought love would adapt itself
to my needs.
But needs grow too fast;
they come up like weeds.
Through cracks in the conversation.
Through silences in the dark.
Through everything you thought was concrete.

Such needful love has to be chopped out
or forced to wilt back,
poisoned by disapproval
from its own soil.

This is bad news, for the conservationist.

My hand shakes before this killing.
My stomach sits jumpy in my chest.
My chest is the Grand Canyon
sprawled empty
over the world.

Whoever he is, he is not worth all this.

And I will never
unclench my teeth long enough
to tell him so.

## *Gift*

He said: Here is my soul.
I did not want his soul
but I am a Southerner
and very polite.
I took it lightly
as it was offered. But did not
chain it down.
I loved it and tended
it. I would hand it back
as good as new.

He said: How dare you want
my soul! Give it back!
How greedy you are!
It is a trait
I had not noticed
before!

I said: But your soul
never left you. It was only
a heavy thought from
your childhood
passed to me for safekeeping.

But he never believed me.
Until the end
he called me possessive
and held his soul
so tightly
it shrank
to fit his hand.

## *At First*

At first I did not fight it.
I *loved* the suffering.
It was being alive!
I felt my heart pump the blood
that splashed my insides
with red flowers:
I savoured my grief
like chilled wine.

I did not know my life
was being shredded
by an expert.

It was my friend Gloria
who saved me. Whose glancc said 'Really,
you've got to be kidding. Other
women have already done this
sort of suffering for you,
or so I thought.'

## *Mississippi Winter IV*

My father and mother both
used to warn me
that 'a whistling woman and a crowing
hen would surely come to
no good end.' And perhaps I should
have listened to them.
But even at the time I knew
that though my end probably might
not
be good
I must whistle
like a woman undaunted
until I reached it.

## *In These Dissenting Times*

I shall write of the old men I knew
And the young men
I loved
And of the gold toothed women
Mighty of arm
Who dragged us all
To church.

## *Women*

They were women then
My mama's generation
Husky of voice — Stout of
Step
With fists as well as
Hands
How they battered down
Doors
And ironed
Starched white
Shirts
How they led
Armies
Headragged Generals
Across mined
Fields
Booby-trapped
Ditches
To discover books
Desks
A place for us
How they knew what we
*Must* know
Without knowing a page
Of it
Themselves.

## *Poem at Thirty-Nine*

How I miss my father.
I wish he had not been
so tired
when I was
born.

Writing deposit slips and checks
I think of him.
He taught me how.
This is the form,
he must have said:
the way it is done.
I learned to see
bits of paper
as a way
to escape
the life he knew
and even in high school
had a savings
account.

He taught me
that telling the truth
did not always mean
a beating;
though many of my truths
must have grieved him
before the end.

How I miss my father!
He cooked like a person
dancing
in a yoga meditation
and craved the voluptuous
sharing
of good food.

Now I look and cook just like him:
my brain light;
tossing this and that
into the pot;
seasoning none of my life
the same way twice; happy to feed
whoever strays my way.

He would have grown
to admire
the woman I've become:
cooking, writing, chopping wood,
staring into the fire.

## *For My Sister Molly Who in the Fifties*

Once made a fairy rooster from
Mashed potatoes
Whose eyes I forget
But green onions were his tail
And his two legs were carrot sticks
A tomato slice his crown.
Who came home on vacation
When the sun was hot
and cooked
and cleaned
And minded least of all
The children's questions
A million or more
Pouring in on her
Who had been to school
And knew (and told us too) that certain
Words were no longer good
And taught me not to say us for we
No matter what 'Sonny said' up the
road.

FOR MY SISTER MOLLY WHO IN THE FIFTIES
Knew Hamlet well and read into the night
And coached me in my songs of Africa
A continent I never knew
But learned to love
Because 'they' she said could carry
A tune
And spoke in accents never heard

In Eatonton.
Who read from *Prose and Poetry*
And loved to read 'Sam McGee from Tennessee'
On nights the fire was burning low
And Christmas wrapped in angel hair
And I for one prayed for snow.

WHO IN THE FIFTIES
Knew all the written things that made
Us laugh and stories by
The hour    Waking up the story buds
Like fruit. Who walked among the flowers
And brought them inside the house
And smelled as good as they
And looked as bright.
Who made dresses, braided
Hair. Moved chairs about
Hung things from walls
Ordered baths
Frowned on wasp bites
And seemed to know the endings
Of all the tales
I had forgot.

WHO OFF INTO THE UNIVERSITY
Went exploring    To London and
To Rotterdam
Prague and to Liberia
Bringing back the news to us

Who knew none of it
But followed
crops and weather
funerals and
Methodist Homecoming;
easter speeches,
*groaning* church.

WHO FOUND ANOTHER WORLD
Another life        With gentlefolk
Far less trusting
And moved and moved and changed
Her name
And sounded precise
When she spoke        And frowned away
Our sloppishness.

WHO SAW US SILENT
Cursed with fear        A love burning
Inexpressible
And sent me money not for me
But for 'College.'
Who saw me grow through letters
The words misspelled        But not
The longing        Stretching
Growth
The tied and twisting
Tongue
Feet no longer bare
Skin no longer burnt against
The cotton.

WHO BECAME SOMEONE OVERHEAD
A light        A thousand watts
Bright and also blinding
And saw my brothers cloddish
And me destined to be
Wayward
My mother remote        My father
A wearisome farmer
With heartbreaking
Nails.

FOR MY SISTER MOLLY WHO IN THE FIFTIES
Found much
Unbearable
Who walked where few had
Understood        and sensed our
Groping after light
And saw some extinguished
And no doubt mourned.

FOR MY SISTER MOLLY WHO IN THE FIFTIES
Left us.

## *I Said to Poetry*

I said to Poetry: 'I'm finished
with you.'
Having to almost die
before some weird light
comes creeping through
is no fun.
'No thank you, Creation,
no muse need apply.
I'm out for good times —
at the very least,
some painless convention.'

Poetry laid back
and played dead
until this morning
I wasn't sad or anything,
only restless.

Poetry said: 'You remember
the desert, and how glad you were
that you have an eye
to see it with? You remember
that, if ever so slightly?'
I said: 'I didn't hear that.
Besides, it's five o'clock in the a.m.
I'm not getting up
in the dark
to talk to you.'

Poetry said: 'But think about the time
you saw the moon
over the small canyon
that you liked much better
than the grand one — and how surprised you were
that the moonlight was green
and you still had
one good eye
to see it with.

Think of that!'

'I'll join the church!' I said,
huffily, turning my face to the wall.
'I'll learn how to pray again!'

'Let me ask you,' said Poetry.
'When you pray, what do you think
you'll see?'

Poetry had me.

'There's no paper
in this room,' I said.
'And that new pen I bought
makes a funny noise.'

'Bullshit,' said Poetry.
'Bullshit,' said I.

# Grace Nichols

From dih pout
of mih mouth
from dih
treacherous
calm of mih
smile
you can tell

I is a long memoried woman

# *Taint*

But I was stolen by men
the colour of my own skin
borne away by men whose heels
had become hoofs
whose hands had turned talons
bearing me down
  to the trail
of darkness.

But I was traded by men
the colour of my own skin
traded like a fowl    like a goat
like a sack of kernels I was
traded
  for beads    for pans
for trinkets?

No it isn't easy to forget
what we refuse to remember

Daily I rinse the taint
of treachery from my mouth

## *One Continent / To Another*

Child of the middle passage womb
push
daughter of a vengeful Chi
she came
  into the new world
birth aching her pain
from one continent/to another

moaning

her belly cry sounding the wind

and after fifty years
she hasn't forgotten
hasn't forgotten
how she had lain there
in her own blood
lain there in her own shit

bleeding memories in the darkness

how she stumbled onto the shore
how the metals dragged her down
how she thirsted ....

But being born a woman
she moved again
knew it was the Black Beginning
though everything said it was
the end

And she went forth with others of her kind
to scythe the earth knowing that bondage
would not fall like poultice from the
children's forehead

But O she grieved for them
walking beadless
in another land

From the darkness within her
from the dimness of previous
incarnations
the Congo surfaced
so did Sierra Leone and the
Gold Coast which she used to tread
searching the horizons for lost
moons
her jigida guarding the crevice
the soft wet forest
between her thighs

Like the yesterday of creation morning
she had imagined this new world to be —
bereft of fecundity

No she wasn't prepared
for the sea that lashed
fire that seared
solid earth that delivered
her up
birds that flew
not wanting to see the utter
rawness of life everywhere

and the men who seed the children
she wasn't prepared for that look
in their eye

that loss of deep man pride

Now she stoops
in green canefields
piecing the life she would lead

## *We the Women*

We the women who toil
unadorn
heads tie with cheap
cotton

We the women who cut
clear fetch dig sing

We the women making
something from this
ache-and-pain-a-me
back-o-hardness

Yet we the women
who praises go unsung
who voices go unheard
who deaths they sweep
aside
as easy as dead leaves

## *Ala*

Face up
they hold her naked body
to the ground
arms and legs spread-eagle
each tie with rope to stake

then they coat her in sweet
molasses and call us out
to see.....the rebel woman

who with a pin
stick the soft mould
of her own child's head

sending the little-new-born
soul winging its way back
to Africa          free

they call us out to see
the fate for all us rebel
women

the slow and painful
picking away of the flesh
by red and pitiless ants

but while the ants feed
and the sun blind her with
his fury
we the women sing and weep
as we work

O Ala
Uzo is due to join you
to return to the pocket
of your womb

Permit her remains to be
laid to rest – for she has
died a painful death

O Ala
Mother who gives and receives
again in death
Gracious one
have sympathy
let her enter
let her rest

## *Sugar Cane*

1
There is something
about sugarcane

He isn't what
he seem —

indifferent hard
and sheathed in blades

his waving arms
is a sign for help

his skin thick
only to protect
the juice inside
himself
2
His colour
is the aura
of jaundice
when he ripe

he shiver
like ague
when it rain

he suffer
from bellywork

burning fever
and delirium

just before
the hurricane
strike
smashing him to pieces

3

Growing up
is an art

he don't have
any control of

it is us
who groom and
weed him

who stick him
in the earth
in the first place

and when he
growing tall

with the help
of the sun
and rain

we feel the
need to strangle
the life

out of him

But either way he can't survive
4
Slowly
pain-
fully
sugar
cane
pushes
his
knotted
joints
upwards
from
the
earth
slowly
pain-
fully
he
comes
to learn
the
truth
about
himself
the
crimes
committed
in
his

name

5

He cast his shadow
to the earth

the wind is
his only mistress

I hear them
moving
in rustling tones

she shakes
his hard reserve

smoothing
stroking
caressing
all his length
shamelessly

I crouch
below them
quietly

## *Love Act*

She enter into his Great House
her see-far looking eyes
unassuming

He fix her with his glassy stare
and feel the thin fire in his blood
awakening

Soon she is the fuel
that keep them all going

He/his mistresswife/and his
children who take to her breasts
like leeches

He want to tower above her
want her to raise her ebony
haunches and when she does
he think she can be trusted
and drinks her in

And his mistresswife
spending her days in rings
of vacant smiling
is glad to be rid of the
loveact

But time pass/es

Her sorcery cut them
like a whip

She hide her triumph
and slowly stir the hate
of poison in

## *Skin-Teeth*

Not every skin-teeth
is a smile 'Massa'

if you see me smiling
when you pass

if you see me bending
when you ask

Know that I smile
know that I bend
only the better
to rise and strike
again

## *I Coming Back*

I coming back Massa
I coming back

mistress of the underworld
I coming back

colour and shape
of all that is evil
I coming back

dog howling outside
yuh window
I coming back

ball-a-fire
and skinless higue
I coming back

hiss in yuh ear
and prick in yuh skin
I coming back

bone in yuh throat
and laugh in yuh skull
I coming back

I coming back Massa
I coming back

## *In My Name*

Heavy with child

belly
an arc
of black moon

I squat over
dry plantain leaves

and command the earth
to receive you

in my name
in my blood

to receive you
my curled bean

my tainted

perfect child

my bastard fruit
my seedling
my sea grape
my strange mulatto
my little bloodling

Let the snake slipping in deep grass
be dumb before you

Let the centipede writhe and shrivel
in its tracks

Let the evil one strangle on his own tongue
even as he sets his eyes upon you

For with my blood
I've cleansed you
and with my tears
I've pooled the river Niger

now my sweet one it is for you to swim

## *Epilogue*

I have crossed an ocean
I have lost my tongue
from the root of the old
one
a new one has sprung

## *Holding My Beads*

Unforgiving as the course of justice
Inerasable as my scars and fate
I am here
a woman ..... with all my lives
strung out like beads
                                        before me
It isn't privilege or pity
that I seek
It isn't reverence or safety
quick happiness or purity
                                        but
the power to be what I am/a woman
charting my own futures/ a woman
holding my beads in my hand

## *Between Women*

We recognise each other
exhilarate in the recognition
of each other
across the kitchen table
we spend hours
reclaiming
obscured from history our mothers
talk about our fondness
for our wombs and lovers

Disappoint
we disappoint each other
use and betray
use and betray each other
sometimes we even choose
to kill each other

But the need to fill
the pages of silence between us
remain

## *Of course when they ask for poems about the 'Realities' of black women*

what they really want
at times
is a specimen
whose heart is in the dust

a mother-of-sufferer
trampled/oppressed
they want a little black blood
undressed
and validation
for the abused stereotype
already in their heads

                    or else they want
                    a perfect song

I say I can write
no poem big enough
to hold the essence

                    of a black woman
                    or a white woman
                    or a green woman

and there are black women
and black women
                    like a contrasting sky
of rainbow spectrum

touch a black woman
you mistake for a rock
and feel her melting
down to fudge
cradle a soft black woman
and burn fingers as you trace
revolution
beneath her woolly hair

and yes we cut bush
to clear paths
for our children
and yes we throw sprat
to catch whale
and yes
if need by we'll trade
a piece-a-pussy
that see the pickney dem
in the grip-a-hungry-belly

still there ain't no
easy belly category

for a black woman
or a white woman
or a green woman

and there are black women
strong and eloquent
and focussed

and there are black women
who somehow always manage to end up
frail victim

and there are black women
considered so dangerous
in South Africa
they prison them away

maybe this poem is to say

that I like to see
we black women
full-of-we-selves walking

crushing out
with each dancing step
the twisted self-negating
history
we've inherited

crushing out
with each dancing step

## *Dust*

Dust has a right to settle
Milk the right to curdle
Cheese the right to turn green
Scum and fungi are rich words.

## *The Body Reclining*

*(With a thought for Walt)*

I sing the body reclining
I sing the throwing back of self
I sing the cushioned head
The fallen arm
The lolling breast
I sing the body reclining
As an indolent continent

I sing the body reclining
I sing the easy breathing ribs
I sing the horizontal neck
I sing the slow-moving blood
Sluggish as a river
In its lower course

I sing the weighing thighs
The idle toes
The liming knees
I sing the body reclining
As a wayward tree

I sing the restful nerve

Those who scrub and scrub
incessantly
corrupt the body
Those who dust and dust

incessantly
also corrupt the body

And are caught in the asylum
Of their own making
Therefore I sing the body reclining

## *Because She Has Come*

Because she has come
with geometrical designs
upon her breasts

Because she has borne five children
and her belly is criss-crossed
with little tongues of fire

Because she has braided her hair
in the cornrow, twisting it upwards
to show her high inner status

Because she has tucked
a bright wrap
about her Nubian brownness

Because she has stained her toes
with the juice of the henna
to attract any number of arrant males

Because she has the good sense
to wear a scarab
to protect her heart

Because she has a pearl
in the middle
of her lower delta

Give her honour
Give her honour, you fools,
Give her honour.

## *On Stars*

Stars are the nipples
of angels
pressed against the face
of heaven.

## *Tapestry*

The long line of blood
and family ties

An African countenance here
A European countenance there
An Amerindian cast of cheek
An Asianic turn of eye
And the tongue's salty accommodation
The tapestry is mine
All the bloodstained prints
The scatterlinks
The grafting strand of crinkled hair
The black persistent blooming.

## *Beauty*

Beauty
is a fat black woman
walking the fields
pressing a breezed
hibiscus
to her cheek
while the sun lights up
her feet

Beauty
is a fat black woman
riding the waves
drifting in happy oblivion
while the sea turns back
to hug her shape

## *Afterword*

The fat black woman
will come out of the forest
brushing vegetations
from the shorn of her hair

flaunting waterpearls
in the bush of her thighs
blushing wet in the morning
                    sunlight

the fat black woman will sigh
there will be an immense joy
in the full of her eye
as she beholds

behold now the fat black woman
who will come out of the forest

when the last of her race
is finally and utterly extinguished

when the wind pushes back the last curtain
of male white blindness

the fat black woman will emerge
and tremblingly fearlessly

stake her claim again

## *Praise Song for My Mother*

You were
water to me
deep and bold and fathoming

You were
moon's eye to me
pull and grained and mantling

You were
sunrise to me
rise and warm and streaming

You were
the fishes red gill to me
the flame tree's spread to me
the crab's leg/the fried plantain smell
                                        replenishing replenishing

Go to your wide futures, you said

# Lorna Goodison

## *My Last Poem*

I once wrote poems
that emerged so fine
with a rough edge for honing
a soft cloth for polishing
and a houseproud eye
I'd pride myself in making them shine.
But in this false winter
with the real cold to come
no, this season's shift
there are no winters here,
well call it what you will but the cold time is here
with its memorial crosses to mark
my father's dying
and me wondering where next year will find me
in whose vineyard toiling,
I gave my son
to a kind woman to keep
and walked down through the valley
on my scarred feet,
across the river
and into the guilty town
in search of bread
but they had closed the bakery down,
so I returned and said child
there was no bread
I'll write you my last poem instead
my last poem is not my best
all things weaken towards the end.
O but it should be laid out

and chronicled, crazy like my life
with a place for all my several lives
daughter, sister, mistress, friend, warrior
wife
and a high holy ending for the blessed
one
me as mother to a man.
There should be a place for
messages and replies
you are too tightly bound, too whole
he said
I loosened my hair and I bled
now you send conflicting signals they said
divided I turned both ways and fled.
There should be a place for all this
but I'm almost at the end of my last poem
and I'm almost a full woman.
I warm my son's clothes
in this cold time
in the deep of my bosom
and I'm afraid of love.
In fact, should it be
that these are false signals I'm receiving
and not a real unqualified ending
I'm going to keep the word love
and use it in my next poem.
I know it's just the wordsmith's failing
to forge a new metal to ring like its rhyme
but I'll keep its fool's gold
for you see it's always bought me time.
And if I write another poem
I'm going to use it

for it has always used me
and if I ever write another poem
I'm going to return that courtesy.

## *Songs For My Son*

### I

My son cries
the cats answer
I hover over his sleeping
suspended on his milk-stained breath
I live in fear of his hurt, his death.
The fear is real
if I close my eyes when it is at its height
I see him curled man-in-miniature asleep.
I hover over his milk-stained breath
and listen for its rise
every one an assurance that he is alive
and if God bargains
I strike a deal with him,
for his life I owe you something, anything
but please let no harm come to him.
The cat cries
my son answers
his sleep is short
his stomach hurts.

### II

They gather from beyond
through the trees they come
gather on the banks of the family river
one by one they raise the keening song
great grandmother Rebecca of the healing hands
Tata Edward, Bucky, and Brownman

my father's lost mother Maria
and now my father
come to sing the birthsong
and Hannah horsewoman to ride me through.
It's a son, a great grand grandson, a man
born to a headstrong, heartfoolish woman.
part the birth waters with river-washed hands
and let the newson through.
woman born of strong-limbed woman
woman born to parents in peacetime
behold your son
flesh of your flesh
your life's work begun.

## III

The midwife
tie-head African woman
fingers like healing-roots
feeds me thyme-tea
to hurry on your coming
summons the appropriate spirits
to witness your crowning,
a knife keen with garlic
to sever you from me
and we'll never smell
its primal top-notes
you or I
without memories of our joining.

## IV

I'll name you Miles I say
for the music, and for coming
a long way
you suck, my womb pulls
the thirst constant
the connection three-way.

# *Mulatta Song – II*

*Mulatta of the loose-sieved hands*
*frail madonna of bloodstained lands*

Yes I am the lady
this is the right door
the house covered in green
the red lantern
the grey and white cats
and the secrets
in the sandalwood box.
You've come seeking
a poem you say
and somebody directed you
this way?
Yet this is the house
of the lady poet
she wears black and heavy silver
there is calm within
when evening comes
she offers you wine
and sometimes her smile
and sometimes herself
but mostly she sits
and sings to herself.

## *The Mulatta as Penelope*

Tonight I'll pull your limbs through small
soft garments
Your head will part my breasts
and you will hear a different heartbeat.
Today we said the real goodbye, he and I
but this time
I will not sit and spin and spin
the door open to let the madness in
till the sailor finally weary
of the sea
returns with tin souvenirs and a claim
to me.
True, I returned from the quayside
my eyes full of sand
and his salt leaving smell
fresh on my hands
But, you're my anchor awhile now
and that goes deep,
I'll sit in the sun and dry my hair
while you sleep.

## *We Are the Women*

We are the women
with thread bags
anchored deep in our bosoms
containing blood agreements
silver coins and cloves of garlic
and an apocrypha
of Nanny's secrets.

We've made peace
with want
if it doesn't kill us
we'll live with it.

We ignore promises
of plenty
we know that old sankey.

We are the ones
who are always waiting
mouth corner white
by sepulchres and
bone yards
for the bodies of our men,
waiting under massa
waiting under massa table
for the trickle down of crumbs.

We are the women
who ban our bellies
with strips from the full moon
our nerves made keen
from hard grieving
worn thin like
silver sixpences.

We've buried our hope
too long
as the anchor to our
navel strings
we are rooting at
the burying spot
we are uncovering
our hope.

## *I Am Becoming My Mother*

Yellow/brown woman
fingers smelling always of onions

My mother raises rare blooms
and waters them with tea
her birth waters sang like rivers
my mother is now me

My mother had a linen dress
the colour of the sky
and stored lace and damask
tablecloths
to pull shame out of her eye.

I am becoming my mother
brown/yellow woman
fingers smelling always of onions.

## *For My Mother (May I Inherit Half Her Strength)*

My mother loved my father
I write this as an absolute
in this my thirtieth year
the year to discard absolutes

he appeared, her fate disguised,
as a sunday player in a cricket match,
he had ridden from a country
one hundred miles south of hers.

She tells me he dressed the part,
visiting dandy, maroon blazer
cream serge pants, seam like razor,
and the beret and the two-tone shoes.

My father stopped to speak to her sister,
till he looked and saw her by the oleander,
sure in the kingdom of my blue-eyed grandmother.
He never played the cricket match that day.

He wooed her with words and he won her.
He had nothing but words to woo her,
On a visit to distant Kingston he wrote,

'I stood on the corner of King Street and looked,
and not one woman in that town was lovely as you.'

My mother was a child of the petite bourgeoisie
studying to be a teacher, she oiled her hands
to hold pens.
My father barely knew his father, his mother died young,
he was a boy who grew with his granny.

My mother's trousseau came by steamer through the snows
of Montreal
where her sisters Albertha of the cheekbones and the
perennial Rose, combed Jewlit backstreets with French-
turned names for Doris' wedding things.

Such a wedding Harvey River, Hanover, had never seen
Who anywhere had seen a veil fifteen chantilly yards long?
and a crepe de chine dress with inlets of silk godettes
and a neck-line clasped with jewelled pins!

And on her wedding day she wept. For it was a brazen bride in those days
who smiled.
and her bouquet looked for the world like a sheaf of wheat
against the unknown of her belly,
a sheaf of wheat backed by maidenhair fern, representing Harvey River
her face washed by something other than river water.

My father made one assertive move, he took the imported cherub down
from the heights of the cake and dropped it in the soft territory
between her breasts ... and she cried.

When I came to know my mother many years later, I
knew her as the figure
who sat at the first thing I learned to read: 'SINGER', and
she breast-fed
my brother while she sewed; and she taught us to read
while she sewed and
she sat in judgement over all our disputes as she sewed.

She could work miracles, she would make a garment from
a square of cloth
in a span that defied time. Or feed twenty people on a
stew made from
fallen-from-the-head cabbage leaves and a carrot and a
cho-cho and a palmful
of meat.

And she rose early and sent us clean into the world and
she went to bed in
the dark, for my father came in always last.

There is a place somewhere where my mother never took
the younger ones
a country where my father with the always smile
my father whom all women loved, who had the perpetual
quality of wonder
given only to a child ... hurt his bride.

Even at his death there was this 'Friend' who stood by her
side,
but my mother is adamant that that has no place in the
memory of
my father.

When he died, she sewed dark dresses for the women
amongst us
and she summoned that walk, straight-backed, that she
gave to us
and buried him dry-eyed.

Just that morning, weeks after
she stood delivering bananas from their skin
singing in that flat hill country voice

she fell down a note to the realization that she did
not have to be brave, just this once
and she cried.

For her hands grown coarse with raising nine children
for her body for twenty years permanently fat
for the time she pawned her machine for my sister's
Senior Cambridge fees
and for the pain she bore with the eyes of a queen

and she cried also because she loved him.

## *For Rosa Parks*

And how was this soft-voiced woman to know
that this 'No'
in answer to the command to rise
would signal the beginning
of the time of walking?
Soft the word
like the closing of some aweful book
a too-long story
with no pauses for reason
but yes, an ending
and the signal to begin the walking.
But the people had walked before
in yoked formations down to Calabar
into the belly of close-ribbed whales
sealed for seasons
and unloaded to walk again
alongside cane stalks tall as men.
No, walking was not new to them.
Saw a woman tie rags to her feet
running red, burnishing the pavements,
a man with no forty acres
just a mule
riding towards Jerusalem
And the children small somnambulists
moving in the before day morning
And the woman who never raised her voice
never lowered her eyes
just kept walking
leading us towards sunrise.

# *Bedspread*

Sometimes in the still
unchanging afternoons
when the memories crowded
hot and hopeless against
her brow
she would seek its cool colours
and signal him to lie down
in his cell.
It is three in the afternoon Nelson
let us rest here together
upon this bank draped in freedom
colour.
It was woven by women with slender
capable hands
accustomed to binding wounds
hands that closed the eyes of
dead children,
that fought for the right to
speak in their own tongues
in their own land
in their own schools.
They wove the bedspread
and knotted notes of hope
in each strand
and selvedged the edges with
ancient blessings
older than any white man's coming
So in the afternoons lying on this
bright bank of blessing

Nelson my husband I meet you in dreams
my beloved much of the world too is
asleep blind to the tyranny and evil
devouring our people.
But, Mandela, you are rock on this sand
harder than any metal
mined in the bowels of this land
you are purer than any
gold tempered by fire
shall we lie here wrapped
in the colours of our free Azania?
They arrested the bedspread.
They and their friends are working
to arrest the dreams in our heads
and the women, accustomed to closing
the eyes of the dead
are weaving cloths still brighter
to drape us in glory in a Free
Azania.

## *Some of My Worst Wounds*

Some of my worst wounds
have healed into poems.
A few well placed
stabs in the back
have released a singing
trapped between my shoulders.
A carrydown
has lent leverage
to the tongue's rise
and betrayals sent words
hurrying home
to toe the line again.

## *O Love You So Fear the Dark*

O love, you so fear the dark
you so accustomed to fighting.
It only seems like the night
but it's a veiled overture to light
It is transitory love, it is passing.
The dagger, love, sheath it.

The bloodied dove, sweet, release it.
There is nothing to fear
It is dark only as your eyes
or my hair
and it is kind love
It leads to light
If you but knew it
Only unarmed will you go through it.

## *Farewell Wild Woman (I)*

I seemed to have put distance
between me and the wild woman
she being certified bad company
Always inviting me to drink
bloody wine from clay cups
and succumb to false promise
in the yes of slim dark men.
Sometimes though when I'm
closing the house down early
and feeling virtuous for living
one more day without falling too low
I think I see her behind the hibiscus
in dresses competing with their red,
and she's spinning a key hung on a
cat's eye ring
and inviting me to go low riding.

## *Farewell Wild Woman (II)*

Sometime in this first half
the wild woman left.
Rumour spreads a story
that bad love killed her
kinder ones swear
that just like that,
she dreamed herself
off precipices
sheer as her dresses.

Only I think I know
where she went,
(I might even have hidden her
myself)
in a priest's hole
at the side of this house
and feed her occasionally
with unscorched bits of memory.

## *Always Homing Now Soul Towards Light*

Always homing now soul towards light,
want like wings beating
against the hold-back of dark.

Above the face of yet another city
bright with bright points of seduction
I hover, and know from having been there
that the lights of cities go under,
their brilliance is not what
this soul is after.
Night swallows the sunset now
the lips of the horizon come together
and there is in all this dark sky
only one thin line of glow.
When the lips close finally
it will seem (be warned)
it will seem like the dark has won.
But it is only the interim
before the true shining comes.
Light is close sometimes,
it seems to burnish my limbs
some nights.
And for wanting it so
I'm a child then
who must sleep with some
small part of light
from a connection above
my head.
Surround us while we sleep, light

encircling
light in rings marrying me to
source.
To me, I say, fold the dark dresses
of your youth
let the silver run like comets'
tails through your hair
For me, I know, the light in me
does not want to be hidden anymore,
anywhere.

# Notes to help your reading

### Still I Rise

6 *sassiness*: self-confidence, pride in myself.

### Equality

14 *wanton*: promiscuous, sexually 'easy'.

### Well

22 *campañero*: comrade.
*cougars*: mountain lions.

### Johann

33 *Teutons*: Germanic – blue-eyed, blond.

### Women

41 *Headragged*: hair tied in rags to form rows.

### For My Sister Molly Who in the Fifties

46 *changed / Her name:* slaves were routinely given the surnames of their owners, and many people, therefore, changed their names to get rid of the master's name. Often people chose

African names instead because they more truly represented who they really were.

47 *cloddish*: dull and stupid.

## One continent / To another

54 *Chi*: a god.
55 *jigida*: small garment.
*fecudity*: fruitfulness; fertility.
56 *seed the children*: fathered.

## Ala

58 *Ala*: goddess of the earth.

## Sugar Cane

60 *sugarcane*: important Caribbean crop.
*aura*: shade.
*jaundice*: illness that turns people yellow.
*ague*: fever.

## Love Act

64 *Great House*: house of the slave master who uses his slaves as sex objects.

## I Coming Back

67 *higue*: mythical figure; an old woman who slips out of her skin to suck the blood of children.

## In My Name

68 *mulatto*: child fathered by a white man and a black slave mother.

## Of course when they ask for poems about the 'Realities' of black women

72 *validation for the abused stereotype*: Nichols argues that people already have a fixed idea, a prejudice about what black women are like and when they ask for a poem they expect to see their stereotypes validated, or proved true.
74 *self-negating*: that reduces oneself to nothing; here, a history that tries to destroy the self-image of black women.

## The Body Reclining

76 *liming*: West Indian expression for standing around, idling away the time.

## Because She Has Come

78 *Nubian*: African; literally from Nubia an area in NE Africa.
*henna*: plant dye for hair and skin.
*scarab*: beetle-shaped brooch engraved with symbols believed to protect the wearer.
*delta*: triangular shape from the fourth Greek letter Δ; here meaning her genitals, the pearl being her clitoris.

## Praise Song For My Mother

82 *plantain*: banana-like fruit, delicious when fried.

## Songs For My Son

88 *birthsong*: songs sung during labour to relax the mother.
*garlic*: has antiseptic qualities. The knife is used to cut the umbilical cord.

## The Mulatta as Penelope

91 *Mulatta*: woman of mixed race.
*Penelope*: in Greek mythology, wife of Odysseus, who set off on a twenty-year adventure chronicled by Homer in *The Odyssey*. She put off her many suitors all that time by saying she must first weave a shroud for her father-in-law, each night unravelling what she had woven that day. She is a symbol of the faithful woman.

## We Are the Women

92 *garlic*: health-giving root, believed to protect against evil.
*apocrypha*: stories of unknown origin.
*sankey*: cliché; the word is based on the title of a book of religious songs and came to mean platitude – an empty idea without real meaning.
93 *ban*: bind.

## For My Mother (May I Inherit Half Her Strength)

96 *petite bourgeoisie*: lower middle class; people aiming to improve their lives by becoming educated professionals.
*trousseau*: wedding clothes.
*chantilly*: fine lace, from the name of the town in France where it was first made.
*godettes*: triangular pieces of material.

97 *cho-cho:* vegetable like a cucumber.

98 *Senior Cambridge fees*: paid for her sister to take 'O' or 'A' level examinations. 'O' level examinations were later replaced by GCSE.

## For Rosa Parks

99 *Rosa Parks*: in 1955 Rosa said 'no' when told to get out of a 'whites-only' seat on a bus in Montgomery, Alabama, USA, where a form of apartheid was enshrined in the law. Following her arrest, all the black people in Montgomery boycotted the buses. Their resistance started a process which led to the Supreme Court ruling the bus segregation laws unconstitutional. This was the start of the successful American Civil Rights Movement lead in the 1960s by Martin Luther King.

*close-ribbed whales*: slave ships.

## Bedspread

101 *colours of our free Azania*: the reference here is to the ideals of the African National Congress (ANC). This group was set up to fight the apartheid regime in South Africa. Azania is their own name for their country and its colours are green, gold and black. Nelson Mandela is a key figure in the ANC and the poem is written from the point of view of his wife Winnie Mandela. It imagines her thoughts of him during his very long imprisonment.

## Some of My Worst Wounds

102 *lent leverage*: enabled her tongue to move.

**O Love You So Fear the Dark**

103 *overture*: offer to allow the light to begin to enter.

**Always Homing Now Soul Towards Light**

106 *interim*: gap between one thing and another.

# Now you have read the poems

## *Keeping a reading log*

As you begin to work through the anthology, you will find that you will need to take notes, jot down ideas and draft poems of your own. It will help you to keep your own reading log to store all this material which you can refer to for coursework assignments. For simplicity of organisation, it would be best to divide your log into sections, just as the anthology is divided. Within each section of your log you will need the following subsections:

Notes on poems generally
Images
Structures
Essay plans
Drafts of your own poems

## *Building up your own poetry anthology*

Many of the study assignments involve you in writing poems. It's very rare to find that you can write an excellent poem on your first attempt. You need to draft and redraft, looking at how to get each word to work to the very best effect. Look at:

- images: are they clear? original? striking?
- sound patterns: do they work?
- line lengths: do they lead the reader through the poem?

When you feel that you are happy with a poem, write it into your own anthology. These poems can be submitted as GCSE coursework.

# Coursework assignments

The assignments are in four groups:

- *Oral assignments*
  This section is a general one and is designed to be used with each group of poems in turn.
- *Assignments on each group of poems*
  This section mirrors the shape of the whole anthology. Each set of assignments is divided into three parts:
  – Personal response
  – Critical response
  – Your own writing
- *Assignments on the whole anthology*
  This is designed to help you think about what the poems have in common and how they differ.
- *Wider reading and assignments*
  This section offers some suggestions of writers whose work you may enjoy and assignments based on this reading.

All these assignments have been designed to support your work in GCSE. Some will help clarify your thoughts about the poems; others are specific pieces of coursework. This section is planned in such a way that you can work through it by yourself, with a friend, or in a small group, or with your teacher.

## Oral assignments

These general assignments may be used with each section in turn. There is a range of suggestions. Some assignments simply help you find your way into each group of poems. Some will help you build up notes and reflections to help with the later written tasks. Others are more demanding and can be used as specific GCSE oral tasks. They are marked with an asterisk*.

You will need to work in pairs and in small groups. It will help if you stay with the same group for all the tasks because you will learn to work together.

You will need to develop the following group skills:

- Try to listen sensitively.
- Give everyone's ideas a fair hearing.
- Don't let others do the work for you.
- Work together to focus on the task.
- Share your ideas generously.
- Don't be shy in offering ideas – there are no right and wrong answers. Your insight will help others.
- Together plan how you will jot down notes of your discussion for later use – one secretary? everyone taking notes?
- Ask one person to lead the discussion and take turns in this important task – it's a very useful skill to learn.
- Always take a few moments at the end to review what you have discussed and to check that you have got the notes complete.

***Assignments***

**1** When you have read each section discuss the poems. Here are some ideas to help you organise the discussion. Take brief notes of your discussion, these will help with later coursework tasks.

- What do you think of these poems? Jot down a few words to record your first response.
- What are the poet's main themes? Can you summarise them in a few words?
- Which poems did you like straight away? Why?
- Which poems are you still puzzling over? Read them together and discuss them. Look at the section 'Introduction: The poems' on page xii for some ideas on how to read them.

**2** Choose one or two of the poems to read aloud. You may need to work in pairs for this as some of the poems need two voices. Concentrate on the sound pattern the poet has created and make sure that your reading lets the pattern shine through.

**3** *You could extend the reading into a talk lasting at least five minutes. Again choose one or two poems that you enjoy. Practise reading them so that a listener will understand and enjoy them. Try them out in your group and take advice from your friends.

Add to the reading some of your own thoughts about the poem(s) such as:

– explaining why you chose it/them
– explaining the images the poet uses
– talking about the sound pattern she has created
– comparing it to other poems in the section which have similar themes or images.

You will need to make notes about all these things and anything else you want to say. It may help you to write it all out as an essay. This could be used as a piece of written coursework. When it comes to giving the talk though, you must not just read out the essay – that would be dull and flat. It's best to make brief notes that you can glance down at from time to time.

**4** Many of the poems are dramatic. You can easily turn them into a play with one or more characters. Try doing an improvisation around one or more poems and discuss what happens when you no longer have the poets' language to enrich the story or the characters.

**5** *This too could develop into an assignment piece if you planned it carefully and developed the characters and the story fully and followed it by a reading of the poem which sparked the idea.

# Assignments on each group of poems

## Maya Angelou

### *Personal response*

#### *Assignment 1*

Read 'Phenomenal Woman' (page 4) and 'Still I Rise' (page 6).

These, like all Angelou's poems, are written to be read out loud. When she reads them aloud she does so slowly, emphasising the rhythm, letting the rhymes echo in our ears. She stands tall and proud and full of confidence in herself. She is celebrating herself, her race and her femaleness.

*Try reading them aloud in pairs and then to the whole class. Aim to use your voice and body language to communicate a sense of pride, delight and defiance.*

*Go on to discuss what Angelou has to say in these two poems.*

Here are some questions to help your discussion. Take notes of the main points you cover because you will be returning to these themes again. Use your reading log to keep your notes together and remember to title them clearly so you can find them easily when you need them.

*Think about 'Phenomenal Woman' first.*

- What is so phenomenal about her?
- Why do you think 'Men themselves have wondered / What they see in me'?
- Do you think she is talking only about herself – is what she says true only of a very few women, or is every woman phenomenal?
- If this poem was called 'Phenomenal Man' what might it

celebrate? What qualities of men do you think are phenomenal?
- Is this poem about inner or outer beauty?

*Now think about 'Still I Rise'.*

- Why does she challenge us with these questions?

> Does my sassiness upset you?
> Why are you beset with gloom?
> 'Cause I walk like I've got oil wells
> Pumping in my living room.
>
> (page 6)

- Look at the verse:

> Out of the hut of history's shame
> I rise
> Up from a past that's rooted in pain
> I rise
> I'm a black ocean, leaping and wide,
> Welling and swelling I bear in the tide.
>
> (page 7)

  What does she mean by 'history's shame'?
- So far these questions have not specifically asked you to think about the fact that Angelou is writing from a black point of view. In 'Still I Rise' she celebrates her race and her history: 'I am the dream and the hope of the slave.'
  Review your discussion so far. What do the poems tell you about her feelings as a black woman?
- Why do you think these poems were chosen as the first two in the anthology?

***Assignment 2***

Read 'The Memory' (page 8) and 'When I Think About Myself' (page 9).

These poems are the first of several in this collection which record the experience of slavery and racism.

*Start to build up a set of notes in your reading log to record what the poets tell you about slavery.*

You will find common threads in all of them. Your notes can form the basis of some creative or factual writing. You will find assignments on this topic in the 'Assignments on the whole anthology', on page 146 and the assignments in 'Wider reading' on page 152. Start your own research on slavery so that you will have done some of the background reading in preparation for these assignments. The wider reading section offers some starting points. Some of the assignments in this section on Walker and Nichols also focus on the issue of slavery.

### *Assignment 3*

Read 'Coleridge Jackson' (page 10), 'Why Are They Happy People?' (page 13) and 'Equality' (page 14).

> Take the blinders from your vision,
> take the padding from your ears,
> and confess you've heard me crying,
> and admit you've seen my tears.
> (page 15)

*Discuss the poems thinking about these questions:*

- What are the 'blinders' and 'padding' on some people's sight and hearing?
- What do the poems tell you about racism?

*Write your own version of Coleridge Jackson's story.*

Angelou says that 'Everybody in the neighborhood wondered' why Coleridge beat his family, but she also gives us an insight into his pain. Imagine you are him and write a letter or a poem in which you explain your behaviour. The final victim in the story is his 'little family'. You could choose, instead, to write from their point of view.

*Discuss your own experience of and ideas about racism.*

- Why are people racist?
- How do you deal with racism if you are subjected to racist abuse or treatment?
- How do you deal with racism if you are aware of someone else suffering racist abuse or treatment?
- How does your school deal with racist incidents?

*Develop this discussion into a piece of writing – maybe guidelines for your class or your school.*

### Assignment 4

Read 'Remembrance' (page 16) and 'Now Long Ago' (page 17).
They are not conventional love poems. Discuss what the poet tells us about her relationships. Is she happy in love? Think about the Maya Angelou she presents in 'Phenomenal Woman' – does she seem to be the same person in these poems?

## Critical response

### Assignment 5: looking at structures

In this section you will produce a short description of the structure of a poem and learn how to quote from poems.

(a) *Start with 'Phenomenal Woman'. Read it silently first and then out loud. Think carefully about the verse structure; the rhyme pattern; the rhythm of the lines and Angelou's use of repetition.*
*Discuss the structure and make notes about the way the poet has organised the poem.*

Here are questions to help.

Pretty women wonder where my
  secret lies. **a**
I'm not cute or built to suit a
  fashion model's size **a**
But when I start to tell them,
  **b**
They think I'm telling lies. **a**
I say, **c**
It's in the reach of my arms, **d**
The span of my hips, **e**
The stride of my step, **d**
The curl of my lips. **e**
I'm a woman **f**
Phenomenally. **g**
Phenomenal woman, **f**
That's me. **g**

Start by spotting all the rhymes. A good way is to give each new sound pattern a different letter like this. What pattern begins to emerge? The verse can be divided into three sections each having its own rhyme pattern.

How does the pattern help to reinforce the meaning?

I walk into a room **a**
Just as cool as you please, **b**
And to a man, **c**
The fellows stand or **d**
Fall down on their knees. **b**
Then they swarm around me, **e**
A hive of honey bees. **b**
I say, **f**
It's the fire in my eyes, **g**
And the flash of my teeth, **h**
The swing in my waist, **i**
And the joy in my feet. **h**
I'm a woman **k**
Phenomenally. **e**
Phenomenal woman, **k**
That's me. **e**

Look at this pattern? Compare it to the first verse. What have they in common?

Men themselves have wondered
What they see in me.
They try so much
But they can't touch
My inner mystery.
When I try to show them
They say they still can't see.
I say,
It's in the arch of my back,
The sun of my smile,
The ride of my breasts,
The grace of my style.
I'm a woman
Phenomenally.
Phenomenal woman,
That's me.

Now look at the rhythm. Some lines are longer than others. Compare this verse with the first two. What features do they have in common?

What is the reason for the difference in line length? Which lines are repeated in each verse? Why?

Now you understand
Just why my head's not bowed.
I don't shout or jump about
Or have to talk real loud.
When you see me passing
It ought to make you proud.
I say,
It's in the click of my heels,
The bend of my hair,
the palm of my hand,
The need for my care.
'Cause I'm a woman
Phenomenally.
Phenomenal woman,
That's me.

Each verse has two sections like this. What have they in common? How would you describe how they work?

(*b*) *Now use the same technique to examine the structure of 'Still I Rise'.*

*What is the effect of the verse structure? rhyme and rhythm patterns? repetition?*

Your notes of your detailed analysis will help you plan a piece of writing.

(c) *Now write a short piece on how the structure of these two poems helps the poet share her ideas and emotions.*

Before you start, discuss the main points you want to make and jot them down. A good way of doing this is in a topic web like this:

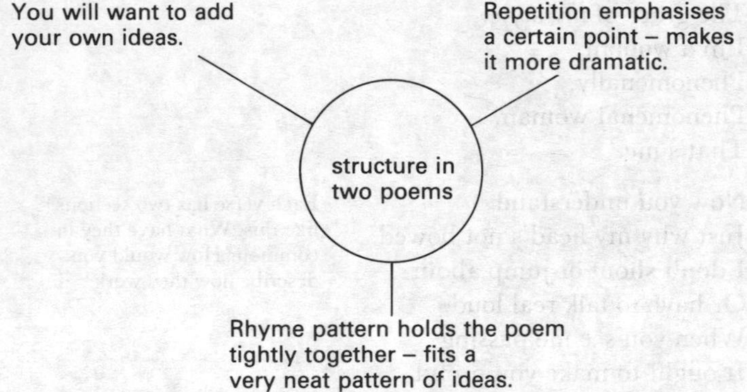


Go through the poems looking for examples of each point you want to make. You will want to quote certain lines to demonstrate a point. For example you might want to talk about Angelou's use of repetition. This is how you would do it.

In both these poems, Angelou uses repetition. In 'Phenomenal Woman' she repeats a similar structure in each verse:

'It's in the reach of my arms,
The span of my hips,
The stride of my step,
The curl of my lips.'
(Verse 1)

and

'It's in the arch of my back,
The sun of my smile,
The ride of my breasts,
The grace of my style.'
(Verse 2)

These lists all have a similar rhythm and a tight rhyme pattern which makes them sound like an incantation or a prayer. They are designed to be read aloud.

- Use colons to indicate you are about to quote.
- Use quote marks to indicate start and finish of quote.
- Lay out the quote so it is clear and separate from your writing.
- Keep the poet's line structure.
- If it helps, indicate which verse you are using.

You might just want to quote the odd word or phrase, in which case you set it out like this:

She stresses her pride in herself even though she's 'not cute' by the repetition of 'Phenomenal woman' in each verse.

Use this writing exercise to practise using quotes and explaining structure. Keep the piece you produce, you will be able to refer to it later.

## *Your own writing*

It is important to know that poets, like you, sometimes can't find just the words they want. Most of the poems in this collection will have been drafted and redrafted many times before the poets were happy with them.

Sometimes you can quickly jot down the framework of a poem, but then it needs working as a skilled woodworker makes a carving. You need to develop images, decide on structures, tune it so that its sound echoes your meaning.

Many ideas and experiences can trigger poems. Here are some arising from Maya Angelou's poetry which might serve as starting points.

**Celebrating me**
What is phenomenal about you? What are you proud of? You don't have to be 'cute'. Think of your strengths and your own 'inner mystery' and write a poem to reward yourself.

**Equality**
One theme of these poems is a demand for equality, between races, between sexes. Use the structure of a poem to record your feelings about equality.

**Poems to read aloud**
You have looked carefully at how some of these poems are designed. Can you use Angelou's technique in a poem of your own? Writing in the style of a poet is one of the best ways of getting to know their work.

# Alice Walker

## *Personal response*

### *Assignment 1*

Read 'Remember? (page 20)

*Discuss the following statements. Which do you think are true, partly true or false?*

– The girl in the poem is powerless.
– The girl in the poem has nothing to do with me.

- The girl and the woman are two different people.
- The poem is about slavery.
- The poem is about the oppression of women.

*Now try to set up some theories about the poem – complete these sentences in your reading log.*

- The girl's eyes and ears are destroyed by...
- The woman is healed by...
- She is listening to...
- Let us begin...

Compare your sentences with those of another group in your class. There is no right or wrong way to finish these sentences. You are trying to explore the spirit of the poem.

Keep the notes of your discussion because the ideas explored in this poem will be echoed in others.

**Assignment 2**

Read 'Well' (page 22).

*Imagine you heard the poetry reading Walker describes. Write a letter, or a poem as she does, to tell the poet how you feel about the images he uses.*

You will need to think carefully about why they stopped smiling when he began to describe the women and what Walker means by:

But what a pity
that
the poet
the priest
and the revolution
never seem
to arrive
for the black woman,
herself.

(page 24)

## *Assignment 3*

Read 'Early Losses: a Requiem' (page 26).
The poem is intended to be read aloud like a story – a simple tale of one person's tragedy. What makes it so poignant is that we know her story is the story of thousands like her.

*Prepare a reading of this poem to present to the class.*

Here are some ideas to help you:

- You might like to add music to enrich your reading.
- You could share the poem among three or four of you. Think carefully about where you might change over voices.
- You could also make a wall display about the harsh facts of the slave trade and use these to help you in a discussion of the poem.

## *Assignment 4*

This assignment is based around a group of poems which have a common theme. They are about the joys and pains of being in love. Read 'Johann' (page 33), 'Did This Happen to Your Mother? Did Your Sister Throw Up a Lot?' (page 36), 'Gift' (page 38) and 'At First' (page 39).

*Working as a group, discuss the poet's handling of this theme in these three poems.*

The last lines of 'At First' could be the starting point for your discussion:

> . . . 'Really,
> you've got to be kidding. Other
> women have already done this
> sort of suffering for you,
> or so I thought.'
>
> (page 39)

– What kind of suffering is Walker describing?
– Have other women gone through this kind of pain?
– Can other people do 'this sort of suffering' for her?

Make notes from your discussion in your reading log.

Now look again at 'Johann' and think about why she fears this relationship.

– Why is 'the Golden Boy, / Shiny but bloody'?
– Why is the combination of 'Blond / And Black... Charged with frenzy / and with blood'?
– Do you think this love has to end in pain? Who will cause the pain?

Go on now to reflect on the ideas you have discussed and to make them your own. Explore them in your own writing – a poem, a story, a play or a letter in which you examine the tensions, joys and suffering which come with love. You may want to think about people of different races, classes or age groups falling in love. You may want to choose your own context or reflect on your own experience or that of someone you know.

### *Assignment 5*

Read 'Mississippi Winter IV' (page 40), 'In These Dissenting Times' (page 40) and 'Women' (page 41).

*Go on to discuss what Walker has to say about the role of women.*

In groups try to agree on three sentences which could represent her ideas. Then discuss whether you agree with her. Match your experience of women against hers. Are there any common principles here?

Keep these notes on women's roles for assignments based on the whole anthology.

### *Assignment 6*

The last two poems in this section are concerned with Walker's memories of two members of her family – her father and her sister. Read 'Poem at Thirty-Nine' (page 42) and 'For My Sister Molly Who in the Fifties' (page 44). She writes about her everyday life and the people who have been important to her. They are ordinary people, but she uses the poems to celebrate their special qualities:

He taught me
that telling the truth
did not always mean
a beating;
though many of my truths
must have grieved him
before the end.

(page 42)

... [She] sensed our
Groping after light
And saw some extinguished
And no doubt mourned.

(page 47)

*Use these poems as springboards for your own reflections on people who may seem ordinary but are remarkable to you. Use whatever vehicle you like to celebrate their everyday achievements – a poem, play or story. You could even write them a letter and tell them why they are so important to you.*

## *Critical response*

### *Assignment 7*

'Early Losses: a Requiem' is a poem particularly rich in imagery. The simple tale of the capture and transportation into slavery is told in a series of powerful word pictures. It is worth dwelling for a while on these images, explaining their meaning and considering how and why Walker achieves the effects she has chosen.

In this assignment you will look closely at some images and prepare to write a short essay in which you reflect on them. There are many images to explore. The ones chosen here will give you some insight into how you might explore the rest.

*Read the poem as a whole from start to finish. Now go through again stopping at each of the sections we look at here. Discuss the questions around each section keeping notes of your ideas. Use these as the basis of an essay.*

*(from verse 3)*
Him I loved as the sun
must seek and chase
its own reflection
across the sky.

Explain this – how and why does she love him?

*(from verse 4)*
Nyanu's dead body
begging remembrance
of his tiny morsel
taken from his mouth.

What is the morsel? What does she mean by 'begging remembrance'?

*(from verse 6)*
our hearts we set
upon each other
as the retreating wave
brings its closest friend
upon its back.

Why is this a particularly good image at this stage in the poem?

*(from verse 7)*
See the savages turn back
my lips
and with hot irons
brand me neck and thigh.

Think this through. What does she mean?

Read the whole of verse 8 and consider what it tells you about how the girl found 'one of you of my own / choice' to love her.

This verse is rich in moving images. Which do you find particularly striking? Spend some time unravelling them and looking at the layers of meaning. Compare how you interpret them with the interpretation of others in your group. A good example of layers of meaning is in this image:

how could I flatten
a wrinkled face?
The stupor of dread
made smooth the look
that to my tormentors
was born erased

Think about why her tormentors think she has no emotions.
Why does she 'erase' the look?

*(from verse 9)*
I shrink to become a tiny size
a delicate morsel
upon my mother's knee
prepared like bread.

Does this remind you of an earlier part of the poem?

PART II
A sound like a small wind
finding the door of a
hollow reed

Use this image as the start of a trail. Go back through the poem and identify other images from nature. There is a pattern woven through the poem. Think about what natural elements she uses to decribe her plight. Why do you think Walker uses these kinds of images in this particular poem?

Now bring together what you have noticed. A good way of doing this is to group your ideas in a topic web like this:

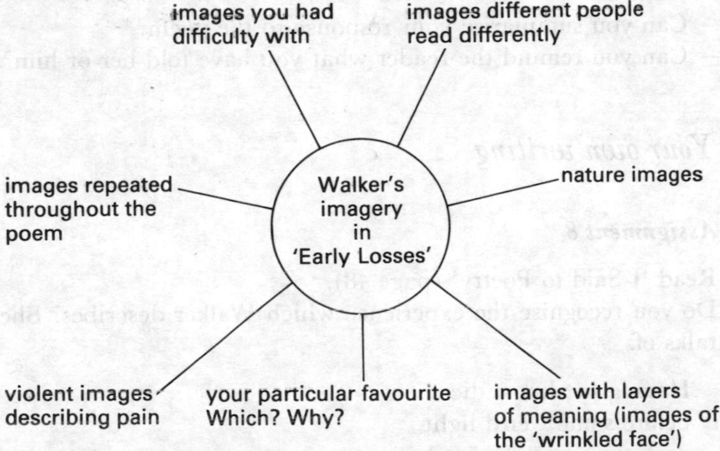


If you have thought through the poem, and discussed it fully you will have many ideas like this. The task now is to group them and work out in which sequence you want to present them in a piece of writing.

*Your essay title is 'Walker's use of imagery in "Early Losses – a Requiem"'.*

Look at the range of what you want to say. Where will you start? Here are some possible starters:
– your own feelings about and response to the poem
– an introduction about the kinds of images Walker uses
– a description of the process you have used to explore the poem and how the meaning emerges as you read, talk and reflect.

Write a first draft of your opening paragraphs and share them with a friend. When you are happy to move on, go back to your topic web and begin to write about each section.

Now think about how you are going to round it off.
- Is there a particular image you want to leave the reader with?
- Can you summarise your response to the poem?
- Can you remind the reader what you have told her or him?

## *Your own writing*

### *Assignment 8*

Read 'I Said to Poetry' (page 48).
Do you recognise the experience which Walker describes? She talks of:

Having to almost die
before some weird light
comes creeping through

Discuss with a friend the process you go through before you can really get into a piece of writing. Do you sit and stare at a blank piece of paper? Do you suddenly remember lots of other things you should be doing instead? Do you find excuses like her?

'... that new pen I bought
makes a funny noise.'

It's good to know that other writers feel as you do. What technique do you use to start writing? Share any good ideas.

Now try your own poem. You can use Walker's title if you like. Try to explore the difficulty of writing and the argument that goes on in your head as you face the task.

# Grace Nichols

## *Personal response*

### *Assignment 1*

Some of the poems in this selection of Nichols' work can be read together. They are the words of 'a long memoried woman' and the story they tell is of slavery, of how women retain their self-respect and find a voice to tell of their lives:

I have crossed an ocean
I have lost my tongue
from the root of the old
one
a new one has sprung
(page 70)

Read these poems:
'From dih pout', (page 52)
'Taint', (page 53)
'One Continent / To Another', (page 54)
'We the Women', (page 57)
'Ala', (page 58)
'Sugar Cane', (page 60)
'Love Act', (page 64)
'Skin-Teeth', (page 66)
'I Coming Back', (page 67)
'In My Name', (page 68)
You may find some of them difficult. For now just try to follow the main ideas Nichols presents.

*Now*

(a) Make notes on what she tells us about how:
- slaves were captured;

- they worked;
- their work on the plantation;
- the white 'massas' treated female slaves.

(b) You can compare this with the poem *Early Losses: a Requiem* by Alice Walker (page 26).

(c) Choose one or two of your favourite poems from the selection for this assignment and prepare a reading of them for another group, another class or an assembly. You may wish to accompany the poetry reading with a short talk about the poetry and why you have chosen it.

(d) Keep your notes in your log for use in later assignments on the whole anthology and on your wider reading.

(e) Extend what you know from the poems by reading more widely about the experience of slavery. Details of useful books are given in 'Assignments based on wider reading' on page 152.

(f) Go on to write a story or a newspaper article about the experience of slavery.

### *Assignment 2*

I say I can write
no poem big enough
to hold the essence
        of a black woman
        or a white woman
        or a green woman
                (page 72)

Most of Grace Nichols' poems in this collection are about women. They are 'full-of-we-selves walking'.

*Read the rest of the poems and discuss how women are presented in them. Make notes of your findings.*

Does it seem unusual to find so many poems about women?

Try a small piece of research. Look at other poetry anthologies in use in your school and make some comparisons. Some will be available in English lessons, others will be in the library.

- Count the number of poems.
- How many are by women?
- How many are about women?
- You could go on to look at the aspects of womens' lives which are considered in the poems you find (political, domestic, sexual, as mothers/daughters/sisters, as workers).

What conclusions do you draw from your research? You can present it initially as a set of figures and then go on to consider reasons why the figures are as they are. You may only have a limited range of anthologies to compare but your information will still be important because it will indicate how much of what has been selected for you to read reflects the lives and concerns of over half the population of the world!

A further piece of research would be to consider how much you get to read about black women and to compare the messages this gives you with Nichols' suspicion, in 'Of course when they ask for poems about the "Realities" of black women', that what people want from her is:

    a specimen
whose heart is in the dust
a mother-of-sufferer
trampled/oppressed
they want a little black blood
undressed
and validation
for the abused stereotype
already in their heads
                or else they want
                a perfect song
                    (page 72)

### *Assignment 3*

Look back at Nichols' work and the notes you made in your discussion in the previous assignment. How do you think she presents black women? Does she offer stereotypes? Look carefully at each poem and consider what each has to say about women. Group together those with similar ideas about women. Do they fit a stereotype? If not, how does she challenge the reader's stereotype?

*Use this as the basis for a piece of writing, 'Black women in Grace Nichols' poetry'.*

## *Critical response*

### *Assignment 4*

In this assignment you will be looking at the decisions a poet makes when structuring a poem. Grace Nichols' work is very fine, very carefully constructed. She uses a verse structure to group sections of each poem and she chooses very carefully how to sequence her ideas. One particular skill is shown in the way she uses the ending of the poem to leave the reader or listener with a very powerful idea or emotion.

To explore the structure of the poems you will need to:

- read each one carefully silently and then aloud;
- focus in your reading on (a) the structure of the verses; (b) Nichols' use of repetition;
- discuss the poems section by section;
- take notes in your reading log of the features you notice.

Start with 'Sugar Cane' (page 60). For each section ask yourself the same question:

- What does the sugar cane have in common with the slave who harvests it?

Then ask specific questions about each section.

*Section 1*

– Why is the last verse longer than the rest?

*Section 2*

– Listen to the sound of this verse:

he shiver
like ague
when it rain

How does the structure of the lines intensify the meaning?

*Section 3*

– Why are there one-line verses?

*Section 4*

– Why is this section made up of such short lines?
– Why is 'pain / fully' divided between two lines?

*Section 5*

– Why is the first line so long?
– Why does the slave only appear in the last verse?

I crouch
below them quietly

You have been thinking about:
– the length of lines;
– the use of verses of different lengths;
– the use of repetition;
– the decisions the poet makes about where to place particular ideas.

Now go on to look at some more poems. This time phrase your own questions about the structure. Build on what you have noticed in 'Sugar Cane'. Read these poems:

'Skin-Teeth' (page 66)
'I Coming Back' (page 67)
'In My Name' (page 68)
'The Body Reclining' (page 76)

'Because She Has Come' (page 78)
Decide on at least two of these to study in detail. When you have read them, discussed them and made notes from your reading and thinking, you are ready to move on.

*Use your ideas and observations to write* either *an essay entitled 'Nichols' craft in structuring her poems'* or *a poem of your own using her techniques.*

You may want to use similar themes or ones of your own. What is important is that you concentrate on applying what she has taught you about structure. It may help if you write a short accompanying piece in which you describe what you have learned and how you attempted to use it in your own work.

### *Assignment 5*

This assignment helps you look at dialect in the poems. Consider these key concepts. A dialect has three features:
– Accent

From dih pout,
of mih mouth
(page 52)

The spelling here tells us the accent in which it is to be read.
– Grammar

I is a long memoried woman
(page 52)

Nichols is using the grammar of a Caribbean dialect.
– Vocabulary
dialects often have their own special vocabulary. In this selection of poems (as in the editorial material of this book) the vocabulary is mostly that of Standard English, but we do get some examples of a West Indian dialect in, for example,

'The Body Reclining' (page 76) where Nichols uses the phrase 'the liming knees' where 'liming' means standing around, idling away the time.

Nichols has the choice of more than one dialect and what is interesting is which one she chooses and why. She may change dialects from one poem to another or even within a poem.

Do your own research. Read your favourite of Grace Nichols' poems and note examples in which she uses non-Standard English, then discuss these statements:

Nichols uses a non-Standard dialect to
- give us the sense of a real person speaking to us;
- change mood – to show sudden anger, pain, humour;
- challenge us – so you thought great poetry had to be written in Standard English?;
- enable herself and her readers to hear her sense of her roots.

Which of these do you agree with? (It's fine to agree with them all.) Can you find examples to support your ideas? Are there other reasons for using non-Standard dialects that you have thought of?

Keep the notes of your discussion for a later assignment based on the work of all four writers.

## *Your own writing*

### *Assignment 6*

Build on your understanding of Nichols' work by trying to write your own poems. Here are some starting points:
- Take one of her themes and match it with your own experience. Suggested titles might be:
  'We the Women'
  'Of course when they ask for poems about the "Realities" of my life' a poem celebrating yourself or someone you know like 'The Body Reclining' or 'Beauty'

- Try writing in a non-Standard dialect as Nichols does, using whichever feels most appropriate. You will have to think about whether to alter the spelling to 'capture' the accent.
- Try grouping your own poems into a collection like this one. You could type them or write them out very carefully so that others could share them.

# Lorna Goodison

## *Personal response*

### *Assignment 1*

The first three of Goodison's poems in this selection are focused around her love for, and celebration of, her son, Miles. She records her love, her 'fear of his hurt' and her joy in her life's centring on him:

> But, you're my anchor awhile now
> and that goes deep,
> (page 91)

Read 'My Last Poem' (page 84), 'Songs For My Son' (page 87), 'The Mulatta as Penelope' (page 91).

Go on to discuss the poems and think about:
- whether you would like a child;
- how you might feel about your child;
- what Goodison tells you about how a mother feels.

You might want to focus especially on 'Songs For My Son'. Look at section II where the poet imagines her ancestors who

> gather on the banks of the family river …
> come to sing the birthsong

Think of your own 'family river' – which of your ancestors sung your birthsong?

Whose voices would you want to hear singing a birthsong for your child?

*Take these discussions and ideas and use them as a starting point for a piece of writing of your own. You can use Goodison's title: 'Songs for My Son'.*

### Assignment 2

Read 'I Am Becoming My Mother' (page 94) and 'For My Mother (May I Inherit Half Her Strength)' (page 95).
One of the strengths of the poems in this collection is that they record and celebrate the lives of ordinary people. Can you use these poems as a springboard for your own writing?

*Choose someone you love and write about how their life has enriched yours.*

### Assignment 3

Read 'For Rosa Parks' (page 99) and 'Bedspread' (page 100).
These poems are about the fight for civil rights in America and South Africa.

Do your own research on Rosa Parks or on the African National Congress (ANC) and the role played in it by Nelson Mandela.

*Bring together what you have learned in an essay, a newspaper article or a talk to your class or an assembly.*

## Critical response

### Assignment 4

Some of my worst wounds
have healed into poems.
(page 102)

Goodison is a brilliant wordsmith. From the threads of her life she weaves a fantastic fabric of words, of images which startle and delight the reader. Her metaphors communicate directly. We 'feel' what she means even before we can consciously unravel her language and explore the images one by one.

*Take one or two of the poems you haven't studied so far and begin to unravel the poet's language and explore the images. Present your findings in an essay on Goodison's use of images.*

Here are some discussion starters on 'Farewell Wild Woman (I)' (page 104) and 'Farewell Wild Woman (II)' (page 105). They are designed to help you think about her images. Use the questions and the ideas you have about her use of language in these poems to help you look at others. (You may, of course, choose to write about these two, but it would probably be best to use the experience you gain in exploring 'Wild Woman' to help you with different ones.)

Read both 'Wild Woman' poems and discuss them.

- Who is the Wild Woman?
- Is Goodison really saying farewell to her?

Look now in detail at both poems. In groups or pairs put the following lines into your own words. When you have finished, compare notes with another group.

(I)
Always inviting me to drink
bloody wine from clay cups ...

... and she's spinning a key hung on a
cat's eye ring
and inviting me to go low riding.

(II)
Sometime in this first half
the wild woman left. ...

... she dreamed herself
off precipices ...

Think about:

- the poet's attitude to the issue;
- whether it is addressed generally or through the viewpoint of one individual;
- the style: imagery; structure; sound patterns; language use;
- what the poet wants the reader/listener to feel or think;
- your personal preferences within the poems on this theme.

Some of the main themes and some poems which illustrate them are listed here to help with your choice.

*Celebrating women*

Maya Angelou
- 'Phenomenal Woman' (page 4)
- 'Still I Rise' (page 6)

Alice Walker
- 'Remember?' (page 20)
- 'Well' (page 22)
- 'Mississippi Winter IV' (page 40)
- 'In These Dissenting Times' (page 40)
- 'Women' (page 41)

Grace Nichols
- 'Holding My Beads' (page 70)
- 'Between Women' (page 71)
- 'Because She Has Come' (page 78)
- 'Beauty' (page 80)

Lorna Goodison
- 'We Are the Women' (page 92)

*Slavery*

Maya Angelou
- 'The Memory' (page 8)
- 'When I Think About Myself' (page 9)

Grace Nichols
- 'Taint' (page 53)
- 'We The Women' (page 57)
- 'Ala' (page 58)
- 'Sugar Cane' (page 60)





(I might even have hidden her
myself) . . .

. . . and feed her occasionally
with unscorched bits of memory.

As you discuss your findings remember that there is no right or wrong answer. We will each interpret a poet's images on the basis of our own experience. All your questions and discussions centre around one main issue. This is 'What does the Wild Woman represent?'.

She is a symbol of something. She represents a whole set of ideas and emotions, just as a dove is a symbol of peace. As you read and discuss other poems consider whether Goodison uses symbols elsewhere.

## *Your own writing*

### Assignment 5

*My Last Poem*

I once wrote poems
that emerged so fine
with a rough edge for honing
a soft cloth for polishing
and a houseproud eye
I'd pride myself in making them shine.

(page 84)

***Use what you have discovered about Goodison's imagery in your own poems. Choose your own theme or borrow one of Goodison's.***

Try to use rich images which emerge 'so fine'. Hone them and polish them until they say what you want.

# Assignments on the whole anthology

### *Assignment 1*

How would you introduce this anthology to another class? It's likely that another group may be studying it at the same time or after your group. Discuss how you would present it to them. Would you:
– talk about it first or start off with a poem?
– discuss why it's worth studying an anthology of poems by black women?
– recommend certain sections or poems?
– take examples of work you have done?
This could be an oral coursework assignment and later could develop into a piece of written work.

### *Assignment 2*

Poems are sound pictures. Plan a poetry reading based on this anthology. Can you visit another group, get an audience in assembly or invite parents to an evening performance? Bearing in mind the time available, select poems which are best read aloud. Practise reading them to do them justice. It might be helpful to prepare a 'handout' for your audience giving them
– titles;
– names of poets;
– notes to help them understand the poems where necessary;
– notes as to why you particularly like each poem.

### *Assignment 3*

Choose your own favourites and make them yours. If you enjoy a particular poem keep a copy of it in the notes you make on the anthology so you can return to it again and again. Learn it off by heart if you really enjoy it, then you can call it to mind whenever you want. Learning poems is very enjoyable and it





enables you to have many, many poets' voices available you in your own writing.

### *Assignment 4*

Make this into a piece of coursework. Choose a group of favourite poems and write a critical appreciation of them. L at:

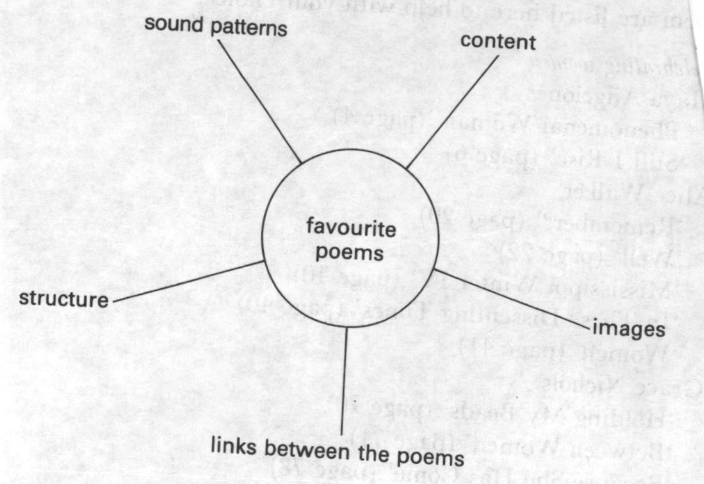


Choose groups, such as poems
– by the same writer;
– on a similar theme;
– using similar techniques.

### *Assignment 5*

Choose one of the themes which runs through this anthology and examine the ways in which it is presented in the different poems.
– What do they have in common?
– How do they differ?

'Love Act' (page 64)
'Skin-Teeth' (page 66)
'I Coming Back' (page 67)
'In My Name' (page 68)

*Black history*
Alice Walker
'Early Losses: a Requiem' (page 26)
Grace Nichols
'One continent / To another' (page 54)
'Epilogue' (page 70)
'Tapestry' (page 79)
'Afterword' (page 81)
Lorna Goodison
'For Rosa Parks' (page 99)
'Bedspread' (page 100)

*Racism*
Maya Angelou
'Coleridge Jackson' (page 10)
'Equality' (page 14)
Grace Nichols
'Of course when they ask for poems about the "Realities" of black women' (page 92)

*Celebrating family*
Alice Walker
'Poem at Thirty-Nine' (page 42)
'For My Sister Molly Who in the Fifties' (page 44)
Grace Nichols
'Praise Song For My Mother' (page 82)
Lorna Goodison
'Songs For My Son' (page 87)
'The Mulatta as Penelope' (page 91)
'I Am Becoming My Mother' (page 94)
'For My Mother (May I Inherit Half Her Strength)' (page 95)

*Sexual love*
Maya Angelou
'Remembrance' (page 16)
'Now Long Ago' (page 17)
Alice Walker
'Johann' (page 33)
'Did This Happen to Your Mother? Did Your Sister Throw Up a Lot?' (page 36)
'Gift' (page 38)
'At First' (page 39)
Lorna Goodison
'O Love You So Fear the Dark' (page 103)

*Writing poetry*
Alice Walker
'I Said To Poetry' (page 48)
Lorna Goodison
'My Last Poem' (page 84)
'Some of My Worst Wounds' (page 102)

## *Assignment 6*

Look at the use of dialect in the poems. The guidelines given in Assignment 5 on page 140 will help you think about this issue. Choose two or three poems which use dialect and discuss why the poet chose a particular dialect and what the dialect contributes to the poem.

# Wider reading

Other publications by the poets in this collection are detailed in the 'Introduction', pages x–xii. There are several other anthologies of women poets which you may enjoy:

*Fire the Sun*, ed. Maura Healy (Longman Modern Women Writers).

*In the Pink* (Women's Press).

*No Holds Barred* (Women's Press).

*The Bloodaxe Book of Contemporary Women Poets*, ed. Jeni Couzyn (Bloodaxe).

*The World Split Open: Women Poets 1552–1950*, ed. Louise Bernikow (Women's Press).

*Watchers and Seekers: Creative Writing by Black Women in Britain*, ed. Cobham & Collins (Women's Press).

*A Dangerous Knowing: Four black women poets*, ed. Barbara Burford (Sheba Feminist Publishers).

*Jamaica Woman*, ed. Mordecai & Morris (Heinemann).

Remember that the poets also write short stories and novels. Here are some short stories and novels with related themes which you may particularly enjoy:

Maya Angelou, *I Know Why The Caged Bird Sings* (Virago).

Alice Walker, *The Colour Purple* (Women's Press).

This anthology has a sister volume, *Quartet of Stories*, ed. Liz Gerschel (Longman Modern Women Writers), which includes the stories of Angelou, Walker, Nichols and Olive Senior. Other relevant volumes in this series include:

Barbara Bleiman (ed.) *Tales for the Telling*, (Longman Modern Women Writers).

Rosa Guy, *Edith Jackson* (Longman Modern Women Writers).

# Assignments based on wider reading

### *Assignment 1*

Assignment 5 on page 147, from the section on the whole anthology, gives you a range of themes introduced and explored in this collection. Take one of them and look at how it is dealt with by one poet here and one writer from the wider reading list on page 151. You could, of course, choose a writer who is not on the list, but who would be suitable for comparison.

### *Assignment 2*

Many of the poems, stories and novels address issues related to black history including the history of slavery.

One of the volumes in the Modern Women Writers Series, *Edith Jackson*, contains an excellent summary of black history by the editor Liz Gerschel. She also suggests some books to read:

Russell L. Adams, *Great Negroes, Past and Present*, (3rd edn) (Afro-Am Publishing Co).
Clayton (ed.), *Martin Luther King: the Peaceful Warrior* (Archway).
Adolph Edwards, *Marcus Garvey* (New Beacon Books).
Roxy Harris, *Being Black: Selections from 'Soledad Brother' and 'Soul on Ice'* (New Beacon Books).
Manning Marable, *Race, Reform and Rebellion: the Second Reconstruction in Black America, 1945–82* (Macmillan). (Although this book is written for adults it is very useful and interesting.)
Alex Haley and Malcolm X, *The Autobiography of Malcolm X* (Grove Press).
Denise Dennis and Susan Willmarth, *Black History for Beginners* (Writers and Readers Publishing Co-operative Society).

Use these resources or others available in your school or local library to research an aspect of black history. Present your research as an article, an essay or a talk to your class using the poems or other fiction reading to illustrate your findings.

### *Assignment 3*

If you can, read the sister volume to this anthology: *Quartet of Stories* in the Longman Modern Women Writers Series. The stories in Liz Gerschel's selection and the poems in this anthology share common themes and concerns.

Look particularly at the stories by Walker, Nichols and Goodison and:

- trace themes which are explored in both stories and poems;
- look at the difference between the writers as they change from poetry to story telling;
- choose favourite poems and stories and explain your choice;
- enjoy the work of Olive Senior and consider how her work compares with the writing of the other three.

## Acknowledgements

We are grateful to the following for permission to reproduce poems:

Karnak House for the author Grace Nichols for 'From dih pout', 'One Continent / to Another', 'We the Women', 'Taint', 'Ala', 'Sugar Cane', 'Holding My Beads', 'Epilogue', 'I Coming Back', 'Love Act', 'In My Name' & 'Skin Teeth' extracted from the original publication *i is a long memoried woman* © Karnak House 1988; New Beacon Books for the author Lorna Goodison for 'My Last Poem', 'We Are the Women', 'Songs for My Son', 'Mulatta Song – II', 'The Mulatta as Penelope', 'I Am Becoming My Mother', 'For Rosa Parks', 'Bedspread' & 'For My Mother (May I Inherit Half Her Strength)' from *I Am Becoming My Mother* (1986) & 'Some of My Worst Wounds', 'O Love You So Fear the Dark', 'Farewell Wild Woman (I)', 'Farewell Wild Woman (II)' & 'Always Homing Soul Towards Light' from *Heartease* (1989) © Lorna Goodison 1986 and 1989; Curtis Brown, the author's agent, on behalf of the author Grace Nichols for 'Between Women', 'I Coming Back' & 'Of course when they ask for poems about the realities of black women' from *Dangerous Knowing* (Sheba Feminist Publishers, 1984) © Grace Nichols, 'Dust', 'The Body Reclining', 'Because She Has come', 'On Stars' & 'Tapestry' from *Lazy Thoughts of a Lazy Woman* (Virago Press) © Grace Nichols 1989, 'A Beauty', 'Afterward' & 'Praise Song for My Mother from *The Fat Black Woman's Poems'* © Grace Nichols 1984; Virago Press for the author Maya Angelou for 'Remembrance', 'Phenomenal Woman', 'And Still I Rise' & 'The Memory' from *And Still I Rise* © Maya Angelou 1986, 'When I think about myself' & 'Now long ago' from *Just Give Me a Cool Drink of Water 'Fore I Diiie* © 1988 Maya Angelou, 'Equality', 'Coleridge Jackson' & 'Why Are They Happy People?' from *I Shall Not Be Moved* © Maya Angelou 1986; The author's agent on behalf of the author Alice Walker for 'Remember?', 'Mississipi Winter IV', 'Poem at 39', I

Said to Poetry' & 'Well' from *Horses Make a Landscape Look More Beautiful* © Alice Walker 1984, 'Johann' from *Once* © Alice Walker 1968, 'In These Dissenting Times', 'Women' & 'For My Sister Molly Who in the 'Fifties' from *Revolutionary Petunias* © Alice Walker 1973 & 'Did This Happen to Your Mother? Did Your Sister Throw Up a Lot?', 'Gift', 'Early Losses: A Requiem, & 'At First' from *Good Night, Willie Lee, I'll See You in the Morning* © Alice Walker 1979 all published by The Women's Press.